ROSSETTI
AND HIS CIRCLE

ROSSETTI
AND HIS CIRCLE

BY

MAX BEERBOHM

A NEW EDITION WITH AN
INTRODUCTION BY

N. JOHN HALL

1987
YALE UNIVERSITY PRESS

NEW HAVEN AND LONDON

Grateful acknowledgment is made to Mrs. Eva Reichmann for permission to publish the Beerbohm drawings and manuscript materials. The twenty-three *Rossetti and His Circle* drawings are reproduced by courtesy of the Trustees of the Tate Gallery; the fresco of Swinburne, Elizabeth Siddal, and Rossetti by courtesy of Merton College Library, Oxford; *Rossetti, in his Back Garden* by courtesy of Birmingham Museums and Art Gallery; *Browning, Taking Tea* and *At the Pines* by courtesy of the Ashmolean Museum, Oxford; *Sophia* and "The Mirror of the Past" manuscript pages by courtesy of the Robert H. Taylor Collection, Princeton University Library; the Lewis Carroll photograph of Rossetti by courtesy of the Trustees of the National Portrait Gallery; the Downey photograph of Scott, Ruskin, and Rossetti by courtesy of the BBC Hulton Picture Library. Other drawings and photographs by courtesy of private collectors. "Further Recollections by Viscount Morley" is published by courtesy of the Taylor Collection.

Library of Congress Cataloging-in-Publication Data

Beerbohm, Max, Sir, 1872–1956.
Rossetti and his circle.

1. Rossetti, Dante Gabriel, 1828–1882—
Caricatures and cartoons.   2. Rossetti, Dante
Gabriel, 1828–1882—Friends and associates—
Caricatures and cartoons.   3. Preraphaelites—
Caricatures and cartoons.   4. English wit and
humor, Pictorial. I. Title.
NC1479.B37A4 1987   741.5'942   87-10539
ISBN 0-300-03986-7

CONTENTS

Introduction. By N. John Hall

ROSSETTI AND HIS CIRCLE

Note. By Max Beerbohm

MORE

Supplementary plates:

AND EVEN MORE

Appendices:

INTRODUCTION

Max Beerbohm once told a friend: "Somehow one doesn't feel sentimental about a period in which oneself has footed it. It is the period that one *didn't* quite know, the period just before oneself, the period of which in earliest days one knew the actual survivors, that lays a really strong hold on one's heart. The magic of the past for me begins at the 'eighties and stretches as far as the 'sixties." For Max, the most intriguing figure of the time just before his own was Dante Gabriel Rossetti, who, as Max said, "shone, for the men and women who knew him, with the ambiguous light of a red torch somewhere in a dense fog." Beerbohm was also attracted by the oddly fascinating people that surrounded Rossetti: painters, poets, writers, models, mistresses, hangers on. Some were geniuses, some had mediocre talents, some were adventurers, almost all were eccentrics—united only in their attraction to Rossetti.

For one familiar with Rossetti's life and work and knowing something of his friends and satellites, there could be no more enlightening and entertaining complement to the memoirs and biographies than Max Beerbohm's *Rossetti and His Circle*, a book of twenty-three caricatures with captions, originally published in 1922. As a satirist, Max frequently remarked that he (generally) mocked only what he loved, and as these drawings move through Rossetti's life they make subtle and affectionate fun of their subjects. Max's temperament demanded that he skirt the tragic and the unseemly in Rossetti's career: he must avoid the still-born child, the suicide of his wife, the debts, depressions, drug addiction, paranoia, near insanity, attempted suicide; the eventual alienation from many of his friends, the sad and relatively early end. But much could be hinted, delicately: Rossetti's compulsive "interest" in women; Fanny Cornforth's ambiguous position as "housekeeper," model, and mistress; his passion for Jane Morris, wife of one of his best friends, whose presence is only suggested in stylized paintings of her hanging in the magical house at 16 Cheyne Walk. Similarly Max can do no more than suggest obliquely Swinburne's sado-masochism or Ruskin's under-developed sexuality. Nonetheless, the twenty-three caricatures tell a great deal. When the book first appeared, *The Times* said, "Each [drawing] is worth a whole volume of sermons on ideals in art and life." Herbert Gorman in the *New York Times* wrote, somewhat optimistically, "Here is the final criticism of the Pre-Raphaelite Brotherhood." One of Rossetti's nieces said that "no person living within [the Pre-Raphaelite] circle had given so accurate a picture of its physical and spiritual composition."

Beerbohm produced the caricatures that became *Rossetti and His Circle* during 1916–17. Having "retired" to Rapallo, Italy, at the time of his marriage in 1910, he returned to England during the Great War. He worked on the drawings in a cottage on the farm of his friend Will Rothenstein in Far Oakridge, Gloucestershire. (Rothenstein's wife Alice was the daughter of W. J. Knewstub, Rossetti's painting assistant in his early Cheyne Walk days.) The Rossetti caricatures were closely related to another project on which Max was engaged in the years just prior to this time: the draft of his second novel (the first, *Zuleika Dobson*, had been a critical success in 1911). This new one, "The Mirror of the Past," like all his fictions, was a blend of fantasy and fact. "The Mirror" is the story of a fictitious character, Sylvester Herringham, who lived for many years near Rossetti in Cheyne Walk, Chelsea. In 1896 he shows Max a mirror that reflects images of what took place in his drawing room years ago. The idea was suggested to Herringham in 1877 by Tennyson when he remarked, "I was thinking how many things that old mirror must have reflected." (Herringham says that Tennyson "had a great command of platitudes—greater even, I always thought, in conversation than in his poems.") Herringham, a scientist, succeeds by 1889 in transforming his mirror, and by the time Max meets him, it is showing, in reverse chronological order, goings-on in his drawing room in 1882. The next year it will reflect 1881, and so on. Max visits Herringham regularly, for some fifteen years, watching Herringham's "Monday Evenings" and listening to the old man's tales of Rossetti and his circle of friends. Herringham dies in 1909, leaving the mirror to Max. When Max moves to Italy, he takes the mirror with him and continues to watch its revelations.

Eventually, Beerbohm gave up on the novel. Science fiction, he decided, was not his forte, and the story got "too complicated." The unfinished novel and the Rossetti caricatures derive from the same impulse. To some extent the drawings could be illustrations to the novel, which itself seems a kind of incomplete prose version of *Rossetti and His Circle*. In 1955, one year before his death, Max salvaged some of the material from "The Mirror of the Past" for a radio broadcast called "Hethway Speaking." Here, changing Herringham's name to Hethway and discarding the device of the mirror, he related some of the stories Herringham had told him about Rossetti and his friends.

In his prefatory Note to *Rossetti and His Circle* Max confesses that he never
set eyes on Rossetti and some of the others, and that those he did meet he
saw only in their old age. Hence he has relied on old drawings, paintings
and photographs.* He has also read about Rossetti and his friends in
various memoirs and biographies. But these had not been his only sources:
"I have had another and surer aid, of the most curious kind imaginable.
And some day I will tell you all about it, if you would care to hear." Until
1982 no one knew what he was talking about, but now Lawrence Danson
has unravelled the mystery in his book *Max Beerbohm and the Mirror of the
Past*, which deciphers and makes sense of the fragmentary and confusing
manuscript of the novel. Max's "surer aid" was Herringham's mirror.

Explaining jokes is a foolish and futile activity. I have attempted only to
provide some of the record without which the reader may miss Max's point.
I have also furnished some of Herringham's especially perceptive
comments. In so doing I have mixed imaginary memoirs with actual ones.
But this was Max's own way: the Rossetti caricatures range from imagined
historical scenes, such as "Rossetti's Courtship," to apocryphal ones, such
as that depicting John Morley's proposal that Rossetti supply colour
illustrations to Mill's *The Subjection of Women*. Moreover, reading the actual
memoirs, one wonders whether the imaginary ones are any less "real." Life
and art blend indistinguishably into each other.

Frontispiece. Rossetti in Childhood

Rossetti's father, Gabriele, had been in turn librettist to the San Carlo
Opera in Naples, assistant curator in the Naples Museum, secretary of the
Department of Public Instruction and Fine Arts at Naples, a member of the
Carbonari—a secret republican society—and eventually the self-styled
"poet of the revolution," "the Tyrtaeus of Italy." He barely escaped King
Ferdinand's murderous persecution of revolutionaries, having been
smuggled out of Naples by an English admiral; after some time in Malta, he

---

*Three such old photographs can be seen in Appendix 1. That taken by William Downey of
Bell Scott, Ruskin, and Rossetti was seen by Max in William Michael Rossetti's *Some
Reminiscences* (Ruskin disliked the picture, terming it a "visible libel"); Downey's photograph
of the Rossettis with Swinburne and Fanny Cornforth Max had in fact not seen, but when
Sydney Cockerell sent it to him in 1923, he wrote back: "Miss Cornforth is incredible . . . and
indeed [I] am but confirmed in a belief I already had—that she must have been just like that
and almost like what (reading between the lines of D. G. R.'s presentments of her) I had made
of her in one of those cartoons [in *Rossetti and His Circle*]." A comparison of old photographs
with the caricatures demonstrates how in *Rossetti and His Circle* Max was working in his later
style in which caricature has somewhat given way to less exaggerated portraiture. Since no
photograph of Sylvester Herringham exists, Max's drawing of him with Rossetti is included.

arrived, in 1824, in London. There Gabriele became professor of Italian at King's College, a post that brought him only £10 per annum; he wrote eccentric books on Dante, on Platonic love, and on himself (a rhyming autobiography). In 1826 he married Frances Mary Lavinia Polidori, a governess, daughter of an Italian teacher and an English governess. Thus the four Rossetti children—Maria, Dante Gabriel, William Michael, and Christina Georgina, born between 1827 and 1830—were by blood only one-fourth English. The Rossetti household in Charlotte Street (today Hallam Street, near Great Portland Street) was altogether Italian. William Michael Rossetti wrote: "It seems hardly an exaggeration to say that every Italian staying in or passing through London, of a Liberal mode of political opinion, sought out my father."

William Michael elaborated on the variousness of Gabriele's guests: counts, barons, generals, plaster cast vendors, coal dealers, organ grinders, prophets, musicians, teachers of Italian, dandies, protestantizing ex-priests, booksellers, coin engravers, dance teachers, poets, piano tuners. Some were not altogether sane. Some were well known, like Paganini the violinist, Ugo Foscolo the writer, Antonio Panizzi, the exile who became Librarian of the British Museum. Many were eccentric, like Marchese Moscati, who believed he had a double stomach and was "a ruminating animal." (Of some, like Benedetto Sangiovanni, a sculptor, William Michael gives a thumbnail sketch: in early youth Sangiovanni had "knifed" someone and come to England with little school learning—Gabriele once narrated to him the story of the Patriarch Joseph, from the Book of Genesis, which came "perfectly new to him, and interested him extremely"; a violently jealous husband, Sangiovanni kept his Anglo-American wife practically a prisoner in Nassau Street, Marylebone, till she, hearing that he had a wife still living in Italy, disappeared with her son to the Mormons in America.) These exiles came to Charlotte Street to talk, and their talk centered largely on their hatred of Louis Philippe, or Luigi Filippo as they called the King of the French. The Rossetti children, William Michael continues, drank in all the talk

as a sort of necessary atmosphere of the daily life, yet with our own little interests and occupations as well—reading, colouring prints, looking into illustrated books. . . I regard it as more than probable that the perpetual excited and of course one-sided talk about Luigi Filippo and other political matters had something to do with the marked alienation from current politics which characterized my brother in his adolescent and adult years. He was not of a long-suffering temper, and may have thought the whole affair a considerable nuisance at times, and resolved that he at least would leave Luigi Filippo and the other potentates of Europe and their ministers, to take care of themselves.

Max's version of Gabriele Rossetti, seated at the table, on the right, follows closely Gabriel's own 1853 drawing of his father, which Max saw reproduced in William Michael's *Memoir*. The figure on the right with raised left arm is a spoof on the main figure in Holman Hunt's *Rienzi* (1849), for which Rossetti himself was the model (in the painting Rienzi, the fourteenth-century Italian revolutionary, is vowing revenge for the death of his brother). Young Gabriel, oblivious to the verbal shot flying overhead, is probably drawing a woman.

1. British Stock and Alien Inspiration

This caricature is the least anecdotal, has the least "narrative" of any in the book. Holman Hunt and John Everett Millais, co-founders with Rossetti of the Pre-Raphaelite Brotherhood in 1848, regard Rossetti in the same way that conservative county members regard Disraeli: "very clever" and "full of wonderful ideas," but "not to be trusted for one moment." The ostensible reason: their Italian and Jewish backgrounds—"Not English!" as Dickens's Mr. Podsnap would have said. Actually, Gabriel grew to be intensely English, while still remaining somehow foreign and exotic and always serving macaroni. He never bothered, for example, to visit Italy: "Why should I go to Italy?" Max has him say in "The Mirror of the Past," "Got it all inside me." The real difference between Hunt and Millais and Rossetti lay in the fact that Rossetti was an intellectual and a literary man, whereas Hunt and Millais were trained painters. There is an irony in Millais's not trusting Rossetti, for it was Millais who eventually violated the chief bond among the Pre-Raphaelite Brotherhood by defecting to the Royal Academy, becoming an Associate in 1853, and Rossetti saw Millais's joining the enemy as the final step in the breakup of the group. Hunt, in one regard at least, would have reason not to trust Rossetti—although as a young man he could not have foreseen that in 1856, while Hunt was away in the Holy Land, Rossetti would get involved with a model named Annie Miller whom Hunt intended to marry on his return. On the other hand, Hunt would later act rather unconventionally himself by marrying his deceased wife's sister (the legal prohibition against such unions, an issue hotly debated for many years in Parliament, was removed only in 1907).

2. Rossetti's Courtship

Elizabeth Siddal, originally Siddall, the great love of Gabriel's young years, was "discovered" in 1850 by his fellow artist and friend Walter Deverell, who found her sewing in a milliner's shop in Leicester Square. A "stupendously beautiful creature," he told Hunt, "like a Queen, magnificently tall, with a lovely figure, a stately neck, and a face of the most delicate and finished modelling . . . she has grey eyes, and her hair is like dazzling copper, and shimmers with lustre." William Michael (in a passage Max apparently read closely) described her as "tall, with a stately throat and fine carriage, pink and white complexion and massive straight coppery-golden hair. Her large greenish-blue eyes, large lidded, were peculiarly noticeable. . . . She maintained an attitude of reserve, self-controlling and alien from approach. Without being prudish . . . she was certainly distant. Her talk was, in my experience, scanty." Lizzie, the daughter of a one-time Sheffield cutler, was soon sitting to various of the Brotherhood painters, but before long she was exclusively Gabriel's model, only partly because she had become seriously ill from lying fully clothed in a tub of water while posing for Millais's *Ophelia*. Gabriel was obsessed with her; he felt "his destiny was defined." By 1852 he had moved into rooms at 14 Chatham Place, overlooking the Thames at Blackfriars Bridge. She was constantly with him, and friends felt they were intruding. He drew her continually. His sister Christina said in a poem that "One face looks out from all his canvasses." She was his Beatrice, his Guinevere. Lizzie herself took up drawing and writing poetry, and Gabriel came to believe she had genius. Ruskin certainly believed she did: he bought up all her drawings, and for a time considered her work superior to Gabriel's. Later Swinburne became a great, almost slavish admirer. (See Supplementary plate 1 reproducing the fresco Max made of Swinburne apparently exhorting Rossetti to do right by her.) The later years of Rossetti's "courtship" were filled with unhappiness, recriminations, separations. She longed for marriage; Gabriel procrastinated; she grew thinner, more ethereal; her health, never strong, deteriorated, largely because of unhappiness over her irregular relationship with Rossetti. He was in the meantime much taken with other models, including Fanny Cornforth, Jane Burden, Annie Miller, and Ruth Herbert.* The courtship struggled on for ten years. In Max's

---

*For Max's sketches of characters of Rossetti's circle, including various models, see "The Mirror of the Past" manuscript pages reproduced in Appendix 2. For most of these figures Max followed illustrations he found in William Michael's *Reminiscences* and the Burne-Jones *Memorials*.

drawing, the mouse may timidly bespeak the squalor of their life; certainly the scattered drawings on the floor reflect the disorder. The figure of Lizzie seems to be loosely based on a now-destroyed drawing of her looking at a canvas by a window in Chatham Place.

3. A Momentary Vision that once befell Young Millais

Millais was a child prodigy who at nine won a silver medal from the Society of Arts, at eleven entered the Royal Academy Schools (the youngest student ever admitted), at fourteen won the medal for drawing from the antique, and at eighteen took the Gold Medal for oil painting. His Pre-Raphaelite period lasted till about 1860 when his work turned toward sentimental, anecdotal paintings and conventional, if technically accomplished, portraits for which Victorian patrons paid so generously. Rossetti considered him an apostate from their early idealistic aims. Part of the explanation for Millais's altered artistic direction lay in the fact that he eventually had a large family to support. He had eight children with Effie Gray, with whom he had fallen in love while painting her husband, John Ruskin. Millais married her in 1855, after her marriage of half a dozen years to Ruskin was annulled for non-consummation. Through his later painting Millais became wealthy, famous, and, at the end of his life, President of the Royal Academy. In Max's drawing, the twenty-year-old Millais is painting, in 1849, his striking Pre-Raphaelite *Ferdinand Lured by Ariel*. The vision that befalls him is of himself in late years dandling on his knee a little girl, an incarnation of his famous oil painting of 1879, *Cherry Ripe*. The model was Edie Ramage, apparelled as she was at a fancy-dress ball organized by the *Graphic* magazine earlier the same year. Her costume was based on that in Reynolds's portrait of Penelope Boothby, and the painting is done in the manner of "Sir Sloshua" (as Rossetti and the Pre-Raphaelites called him). Edie's uncle, William Thomas, editor of the *Graphic*, paid Millais 1,000 guineas for the painting, which was then reproduced in chromolithography as a supplement to the *Graphic* in 1880. It reportedly sold 600,000 copies.

4. A Remark by Benjamin Jowett

In 1857 at the beginning of the Long Vacation at Oxford, Rossetti was inspecting the new University Museum and the new Oxford Union

Debating Hall, both designed by his friend Benjamin Woodward. In the latter building, in a gallery running round the hall, Rossetti saw ten bays, each pierced by two circular windows; he immediately offered to decorate these bays with paintings, gratis, asking only for expenses. The interim Union Committee accepted his proposal, and Rossetti enlisted the help of his latest disciples, foremost among whom were two men he had met the previous year when they were Oxford undergraduates, Edward Burne-Jones and William Morris—Ned and Topsy as they were familiarly known. His older painter friends, Brown, Hunt, and Scott, were unwilling or unable to assist in the project, but other young men did: Val Prinsep, Spencer Stanhope, Hungerford Pollen, Arthur Hughes. Prinsep tells how he hesitated, alleging his deficiencies in drawing, to which Rossetti replied: "Nonsense, there's a man I know who has never painted anything—his name is Morris—he has undertaken one of the panels and he will do something very good you may depend—so you had better come." The time Rossetti spent painting the Oxford murals, in the company of his new band of young acolytes, the "jovial campaign" as he called it, was probably the happiest of his life. Released from the ailing Lizzie, he entered into a kind of carefree undergraduate life, delighting in the camaraderie of the painters, with their long hours of talk about art, their practical jokes, clowning, emptying of pots of paint on one another from atop scaffolds. This delicious time lasted for Rossetti only two months, after which he was urgently summoned back to Lizzie, whose condition had now worsened. He left his mural unfinished, and it remained so in spite of his intention to return and complete it. The tempera paint was applied to scarcely dry walls and within less than a year had begun to flake off or fade into the surface. Gabriel's work, which Ruskin had called "the finest piece of colour in the world," pretty much disappeared.

All the murals were scenes from Malory's *Morte D'Arthur*: Rossetti chose *Sir Launcelot's Vision of the Sanc Grael*, in which, as he explained, "Sir Launcelot [is] prevented by his sin from entering the chapel of the San Grail. He has fallen asleep before the shrine full of angels, and, between him and it, rises in his dream the image of Queen Guinevere, the cause of all. She stands gazing at him with her arms extended in the branches of an apple-tree." Max drew his version from a reproduction of a preliminary drawing by Rossetti in the Burne-Jones *Memorials* (Burne-Jones himself sat for Launcelot). In the early sketches Guinevere was Lizzie; in later ones, and in the actual mural, she was Jane Burden, whom Rossetti had first seen in a theatre box at Oxford. She was a "stunner" of seventeen, a local girl, the daughter of a stableman. Legend says that Rossetti fell in love with her and would have married her had he not been guiltily committed to Lizzie, and that he encouraged Morris to marry her in order to keep her in the Rossetti circle. Whatever the truth, Morris married Jane Burden in April 1859. She was to be the great love and passion of Rossetti's last fifteen years, the sitter for many of his paintings, and the compelling force behind much of his love poetry.

The memoirs show that the Bohemian painters and the university men did not mix well; and Max, for his depiction of this segment of Rossetti's career, chose an imaginary encounter between the painter and Benjamin Jowett, noted Professor of Greek. (Max made Jowett, born in 1817, older than his years.) At the time Jowett was still sorely disappointed at not having been elected Master of Balliol—he was elected in 1870 and later became Vice-Chancellor of the University. Jowett, a short, thin man, was known for his wry and cutting wit. He is on record as disliking the Pre-Raphaelites, and he believed that their influence had done much to ruin the college career of a young Balliol undergraduate, Algernon Charles Swinburne, who, during the mural-painting campaign, had joined Rossetti's other young followers. It was also at Oxford that Rossetti met still another undergraduate admirer, Sylvester Herringham.

5. COVENTRY PATMORE AT SPRING COTTAGE

On 23 May 1860 Rossetti, after ten years of "courtship," finally married Lizzie. Her failing health had perhaps made him fear for her life. After a spiritless trip to Paris, they took rooms in Spring Cottage, Downshire Hill, Hampstead, a neighbourhood they thought would be better for her health than the damp, foggy riverfront of Chatham Place. The poet Coventry Patmore, who had known Rossetti since 1849, had been the only published writer to contribute to the short-lived Pre-Raphaelite magazine, *The Germ*. It was Patmore who persuaded John Ruskin to publish two letters in *The Times* in May 1851 defending the Pre-Raphaelites when the art world seemed almost universally against them. And at the close of 1857 Patmore had written an enthusiastic article on the Oxford Union wall paintings, declaring Gabriel "the only modern rival of Turner as a colourist." In Max's caricature, Patmore is preaching domesticity to the apparently bored and unimpressed newlyweds. The very names of Patmore's books of poetry celebrating wedded love make an ironic commentary on Rossetti's situation: *The Angel in the House: The Betrothal* (1854), *The Espousals* (1856), *Faithful for Ever* (1860), and *The Victories of Love* (1862). After a few months in Hampstead, Gabriel and Lizzie moved back to Chatham Place.

6. NED JONES AND TOPSY

In 1856 (Max occasionally disregards chronological order) Morris and
Burne-Jones, up in London from Oxford, under Rossetti's spell and
determined to make a life in art, were persuaded by him to take three rooms
on the first floor of 17 Red Lion Square, the very rooms that Rossetti and
Walter Deverell had occupied earlier. Max's drawing took its inspiration
from a passage in Mackail's *Life of William Morris*:

> The rooms in Red Lion Square were unfurnished: and from this trifling
> circumstance came the beginnings of Morris's work as a decorator and
> manufacturer. . . . Morris [made] rough drawings of the things he most
> wanted, and then [got] a carpenter in the neighbourhood to construct
> them from those drawings in plain deal. Thus the rooms in Red Lion
> Square were gradually provided with "intensely mediaeval furniture" as
> Rossetti described it, "tables and chairs like incubi and succubi". . . .
> Afterwards a large settle was designed, with a long seat below, and above
> three cupboards with great swing doors. "There were many scenes with
> the carpenter," Sir Edward Burne-Jones says: "especially I remember the
> night when the settle came home. We were out when it reached the house,
> but when we came in, all the passages and the staircase were choked with
> vast blocks of timber, and there was a scene. I think the measurements had
> perhaps been given a little wrongly, and that it was bigger altogether than
> he had ever meant, but set up it was finally, and our studio was one-third
> less in size. Rossetti came. This was always a terrifying moment to the very
> last. He laughed, but approved." Not only so, but he at once made designs
> for oil paintings to be executed on the panels of the cupboard doors and
> the sides of the settle.

Morris, Sylvester Herringham recalled, gave Rossetti none of "the
poetical adoration of Swinburne or Ned Jones—more of the brisk deference
of bosun to skipper, or foreman to superintendent." Morris, he said, was
interested in things: "For a man who doesn't like machinery, Top is
surprisingly like a steam engine."

Of all the followers of Rossetti—except Hall Caine—Max seems to have
had least regard for Morris. In a lengthy letter in 1913, thanking Holbrook
Jackson for dedicating his book on the 1890s to him, Beerbohm said that he
thought Jackson overrated Morris:

> He is splendid, certainly, by reason of the bulk and variety of his work, but
> when it comes to the quality of any part of that work—Here again I leave
> a wide margin (I am glad Morris isn't alive to fill in the margin with

decorations) for my necessary injustice. I like in visual objects a lightness and severity, blitheness and simplicity. A gloomy complexity is no doubt equally a noble thing to strive for. Morris achieved it in his wall-papers. . . . [The Kelmscott books] seem to me a monument of barren and lumbering affectation: not *books* at all; for books, to be alive and to deserve their title, must be printed in such wise that the contemporary reader can forget the printing and be in direct touch with the author's meaning. Morris' pseudo-mediaevalism utterly prevents—but there, there. I am boring your head off, and my letter is so long that you will be sorry you ever dedicated your book to me.

For an account of Morris's attempt, along with his partner Charles Faulkner, to redecorate Sylvester Herringham's drawing room, see Appendix 3.

7. John Ruskin meets Miss Cornforth

Four years Rossetti's senior and almost illiterate, Fanny Cornforth was a country girl whose real name was Sarah Cox. She adopted the name of her grandmother on coming up to London, where she became a prostitute. Her first meeting with Rossetti took place some time in the late 1850s; one story has Fanny standing in the Strand "cracking nuts with her teeth" and throwing the shells at Rossetti, who then asked her to model. Her version was that while she was walking with an elderly cousin in Surrey Gardens, Rossetti deliberately contrived to collide with her, loosing her mass of golden hair; he then apologized and persuaded her to model for him. She cast a spell over Rossetti that most of his friends resented. She was vulgar, ineducable, coarse, and voluptuous, certainly the opposite of the ethereal, artistic Lizzie. Indeed the antithesis between the two women explains much of her attraction for Rossetti. When, after Lizzie's death in 1862, Rossetti moved into 16 Cheyne Walk, Fanny, whom he set up in lodgings nearby, became his "housekeeper," model, and mistress. Her reign as favorite model lasted only a few years, but she remained a part of Rossetti's life until the end; she was one of the few people whom Rossetti made it his business to take care of, to be responsible for. Usually others were taking care of him. Fanny, the only Rossetti model who refused even to attempt to enter into the world of art and poetry that Rossetti and his friends lived for, was an embarrassment, and she was frequently ushered out of the way when visitors called. In Max's picture, Rossetti seems to have been trapped into introducing her to Ruskin, who had so doted upon Lizzie, whose

portrait hangs in the background. The husky Fanny also contrasts nicely
with the narrow-shouldered, thin Ruskin (William Michael said, "I have
sometimes laid a light grasp on his coat-sleeve, and there seemed to be next
to nothing inside it").

Fanny grew increasingly fat. William Bell Scott referred to her as "that
three waisted creature," and Rossetti himself affectionately called her
"Elephant." Max, late in life, told Samuel Behrman that he preferred the
healthy Fanny Cornforth to the doomed Elizabeth Siddal: "It must have
been hard work for the Pre-Raphaelites to be constantly ethereal, and Miss
Cornforth was bosomy and earthy. She afforded the Pre-Raphaelites a nice
change from Pre-Raphaelitism; she was Rubensy." In some ways Fanny
was like the little-known Mildred Crump, Rossetti's model in 1865 for a
painting called *Lilies that Fester*. Sylvester Herringham bought the painting
and married the girl. As Herringham told Max: "I doubt if but for
[Rossetti] I should ever have married her—or any one. I have told you
what an influence he was for all men who knew him. Consciously or
unconsciously everyone was affected by him." Rossetti had scoffed at the
idea of Herringham's attraction to young "ladies," calling them "bread
and butter misses—*thin slices*—swallow a dozen of them, unsatisfied"; he
said that "women of humble class alone could inspire passion—they were
natural—they had mystery—they inspire pity. King Cophetua. Imagine
Lizzie a lady! Or Janey! Not that they didn't beat *ladies* at their own game.
Easy thing to pick up at any moment at right age." Then Mildred, after
two years, eloped with one Lord Runcorn, to whom she had been
introduced by the mischievous Charles Augustus Howell (of whom more
below). The incensed and broken-hearted Herringham destroyed
Rossetti's *Lilies that Fester*, an act that caused the two friends to fall out.
Herringham protested that of all men Rossetti, who had buried his own
manuscript poems with his dead wife, should understand. But Rossetti said
that "a man . . . may sacrifice his work for a woman. Not another man's."

8. Blue China

"Jimmy" Whistler was Rossetti's neighbour in Chelsea, and for a long time
they were friends. They vied passionately with each other in collecting blue
china. Rossetti for a few years had a positive mania for "pots." There
survives in various forms the story of Rossetti dining at a friend's and
unthinkingly turning over a plate full of food to inspect its mark. Another

story has Rossetti stealing a valuable plate from Howell, who in turn contrived to steal it back.

In Max's caricature of Whistler enthusiastically explaining a vase of blue Nankin china to a dour and doubtful Carlyle, the drawing of Carlyle seems to parody Whistler's famous *Arrangement in Grey and Black No. 2*. Max was fascinated by the idea of Carlyle sitting to Whistler, and in the very pose in which Whistler had painted his mother. Herringham was able to explain how it came about:

Since Mrs. Carlyle's death [Carlyle] had formed the habit of going often to Madame Venturi's house. He may have thought her a poor crittur, but she loved Janie's memory, and that sufficed. "And one day," he told me, "there was a wee young man with a mop of black ringlets and a quizzing-glass—a sor-rt of pocket D'Israeli by the looks of him, but American in his talk, of which there was much. When he was gone, Mrs. Venturi asked me what I thought of him; and I told her without cir-r-cumlocution. Said she, But he's going to be a verra great painter, and he wants to paint you; and he's verra poor, she said: and he's verra guid to his Mither-r. She's a most per-rtinaceous crittur, is Mrs. Venturi, and next day I found myself with her at a house alongside the river, there to see this Mr. Whistler's paintings. The Mither-r received us—a dainty-sad little auld silvery dame, gentle of speech and shy-authoritative. Presently in comes son, and we all go into his wor-rk-room, and there, propped up on a bit of wooden stand, is a picture of the Mither-r with a frame to it. There she sat, side-face, a sad figure, all in black, lonesome and shy-authoritative, against a plain grey wall of parlour. I canna count how many sittings I gave that slow-working son. One day he said finis and showed me his handiwork. There I sat, side-face, all in black, lonesome and meditative-gentle, against pale grey wall of parlour. Painter stood by me sharp-expectant. 'Well, young man,' I said at last, 'ye're verra filial, verra filial indeed.'"

Herringham went on to contrast Carlyle with Ruskin. He said that teaching or preaching geniuses always had messages "characteristic of the messengers," of whom he discerned two kinds, "the vain ones who want us to be just like themselves; and the modest ones who would have us be just what they are not.... Mr. Carlyle, for all his faults of temper, was one of the modest kind, and Mr. Ruskin—generous and usually angelic though he was—was one of the vain. Mr. Carlyle, being eloquent, and a peasant, and always ailing, desiderated a race of strong silent aristocrats; and dear Mr. Ruskin despaired of a world in which not everybody admired Giotto and Turner and Miss Kate Greenaway as much as he."

In Max's drawing, Carlyle, in crumpled coat and holding a battered hat, stands temporarily mute before Whistler, dandy from tip to toe. Max, himself a consummate dandy, said of Carlyle's *Sartor Resartus*: "That anyone who dressed so very badly as did Thomas Carlyle should have tried to construct a philosophy of clothes has always seemed to me one of the most pathetic things in literature. He in the Temple of Vestments! Why sought he to intrude, another Clodius, upon those mysteries and light his pipe from those ardent censers? What were his hobnails that they should mar the pavement of that delicate Temple?"

9. WOOLNER AT FARRINGFORD

Mrs. Tennyson, the former Emily Sellwood, whom Tennyson had married in 1850 (the same year in which he was appointed Poet Laureate), brought order into Tennyson's rather untidy life. She arranged his appointments and social life; she saw that bills were paid and letters answered. She was also involved in his work, sometimes deciding upon subjects for his poems and even providing prose versions beforehand; she had a say in determining the titles of his books and entered into his negotiations with publishers. Some people claimed she tamed his poetry. There is no doubt that she worshipped him and his work, and as he was most susceptible to praise and sensitive to criticism, she was in some respects the perfect spouse. Tennyson was a difficult person—Edward Lear said he believed "no other woman in all this world could live with him for a month."

From the time of her marriage, Mrs. Tennyson had taken a special liking to Thomas Woolner, a young sculptor, and he became a close family friend. However egotistical, outspoken and dogmatic some others found him, Emily Tennyson was his champion. Woolner genuinely admired Tennyson and did not hesitate to tell Mrs. Tennyson as much; in his letters to her he calls the poet "divine" and "glorious and mighty among men." Woolner, one of the seven original Pre-Raphaelites, had been unsuccessful as a sculptor, although his 1850 portrait medallion of Tennyson was well regarded. He had sailed for Australia in 1852, having stayed his last two days with the Tennysons; but the colonies proved unlucrative, and Woolner was back in England two years later. Through Mrs. Tennyson's influence he was able to sculpt a second medallion of Tennyson; she reported her husband pleased with a preliminary version; she herself liked it but did suggest "the scraping away of a little of the nose underneath the nostril all along to the point so as to shorten the nose a wee bit." Woolner complied. Emily then conspired with Woolner in a much more ambitious project, a sculpted bust of the poet. It took some doing, for Tennyson, as Woolner said, anticipated the operation "with shoulder-shrugging horror." Emily counseled Woolner, "We must catch him as we can for the few sittings you will want. I hope it may be warm enough for us in the drawing-room for I fear the study would not be so good a light for you." The sittings took place during five weeks in February and March 1856 at Farringford, Tennyson's home on the Isle of Wight. Emily's journal recorded: "Difficult work for Mr. Woolner as A. is not at all fond of having his face copied & will only spare a little while at night when Mr. Woolner has to take a candle in one hand & model as he can." The bust, which showed Tennyson considerably younger than his years, was completed in March 1857. Millais, according to Woolner, "went quite into raptures at the sight of it"; Carlyle called it a "thorough success"; Ruskin, at least at first, thought it "a triumph of Art." The work was the turning point in Woolner's career. An American tried to buy the bust, but the Tennysons objected and were pleased when it was eventually purchased for the Library of Trinity College, Cambridge. There had been some difficulty at first, but Vernon Lushington, Woolner's advocate with the college authorities, reported to him in November 1859: "Good news. The mighty Master & his men have at last graciously condescended to accept your *Masterpiece*, & even with thanks. Into the College Library itself they won't allow it to go, that being devoted to the dead men, but they offer it place in the *Vestibule* of the Library, to be promoted we hope, in due time, when old Tennyson himself is promoted." Woolner carved two replicas, one of which was eventually enshrined in Poets' Corner, Westminster Abbey. The original has not been "promoted" to the Trinity College Library proper but is situated in a corridor leading to the New Library and next to the gentlemen's lavatory.

Tennyson was quite vain (the wall in Max's drawing is filled with likenesses of him) and excessively fond of reading his poetry aloud to whatever listeners he could corner. Rossetti, who had been introduced to Tennyson by Coventry Patmore in 1849, was subjected to one of the Laureate's readings of *Maud* in its entirety—a two to three hour performance—when he called on the Brownings in London in September 1855. Gabriel, who was not enamoured of *Maud*, having found it "an odd De Balzackish sort of story for an Englishman at Tennyson's age" and in places "very like rubbish," sat bored and sketching a caricature of

Tennyson, who, as he read, would interrupt himself occasionally: "There's a wonderful touch! That's very tender! How beautiful that is!" as tears streamed down his face.

Upon Prince Albert's sudden death in 1861, Tennyson quickly added a "Dedication" in his memory to the new edition of the *Idylls of the King* (the idea may have been Emily's). The Queen, according to Princess Alice, was consoled somewhat by this gesture. That Albert had greatly admired Tennyson's work must have rendered *In Memoriam* all the more a favorite with the grief-stricken Queen. By March 1862 Tennyson was summoned to Osborne; he was so unnerved by the interview that he could later recall little except that he had blurted out "What an excellent King Prince Albert would have made," a remark he immediately regretted. Luckily the Queen took no offense, but rather agreed with him. Thereafter Tennyson was called to Osborne at various times and exchanged frequent letters with her. Tennyson never read *In Memoriam* to his Sovereign (Supplementary plate 2), although Max's cartoon, first published in 1904 in *The Poets' Corner*, became so popular that some people have believed it records an actual occurrence. In fact, something very much the opposite of what Max depicted is closer to the truth: during an interview at Osborne on 7 August 1883, the Queen twice quoted *In Memoriam* to Tennyson. One of her excerpts was prompted by their discussion of whether in the afterlife they would be able to recognize old friends. Tennyson expressed his doubts, recounting how his dog had once failed to know him when he came naked from bathing. She countered with a passage from *In Memoriam* ending "And I shall know him when we meet."

10. FORD MADOX BROWN PATRONISED BY HOLMAN HUNT

Ford Madox Brown, a painter six years older than Rossetti, met him in 1848 and remained his close friend always. At their first meeting Brown offered to give him lessons, free. Rossetti, however, quickly grew tired of exercises in drawing and painting pickle jars and medicine bottles. He then put himself briefly under the tutelage of Holman Hunt, a young man just one year his senior. "Old Brown" was never a commercial success, and he was sometimes a despondent figure, fussing endlessly over his work and continually overpainting. Moreover, Ruskin, who so helpfully championed the Pre-Raphaelites, was antipathetic to Brown's work. Hunt, on the other hand, eventually gained much popularity, especially after the enormously successful Simmons and Ridgeway engravings of his *Light of the World*. Max read Hunt's garrulous two-volume autobiography—"a finely solid and (between the lines) delightful production" he calls it—a work devoted largely to showing that he himself had been the leader of the Pre-Raphaelites. Hunt had become increasingly jealous of Rossetti's posthumous celebrity and displeased by the many accounts of the Brotherhood, all of which featured Rossetti. He must have been especially annoyed by Hall Caine's claim that Rossetti rather debunked the whole thing, saying, "What you call a movement was serious enough, but the banding together under the title was all a joke. We had at that time a phenomenal antipathy to the Academy, and in sheer love of being outlawed signed our pictures with the well-known initials." The Brotherhood was "the mere affectation of a parcel of boys." And again: "Pre-Raphaelites! A group of young fellows who couldn't draw!" (Rossetti himself realized that he had not been able to execute "Pre-Raphaelite" paintings as well as Millais and Hunt, and it was in his interest to play down the days of the Brotherhood.) Caine also quoted Rossetti as saying that there was no such thing as an "English school" of painting, that not even the Pre-Raphaelites could claim such a title, but that if anyone did start an English school, it was Brown: "And he's more French than English. Hunt and Jones have no more claim to it than I have." Hunt in his book was therefore at great pains to demolish the "ingenious theory" that Brown was in some way the "grandfather" of the Pre-Raphaelites. Hunt explained, for example, that he had vetoed the very idea of inviting Brown to join the Brotherhood, alleging the unsuitability of Brown's German anti-quarianism, his "grim grotesqueness of invention" and "startling crochets."

The figure of the child in Max's caricature is derived from Brown's *The English Boy*, a portrait of his precocious son Oliver.

11. The Small Hours in the 'Sixties at 16, Cheyne Walk

In late October 1862 Rossetti moved into 16 Cheyne Walk, Chelsea, a large, comfortable, red brick building that was called "Tudor House" and "The Queen's House" because Queen Catherine Parr was said to have retired there after the death of Henry VIII. It was to be Rossetti's home until his death twenty years later. Swinburne, now a great friend, was joint tenant, with George Meredith and William Michael staying there some evenings and also contributing to the rent. Meredith lasted only a few months, Swinburne about a year. The accommodating and noncombative William stayed on as part-tenant till 1869. Rossetti, always a spendthrift, fitted out the house with lovely old furniture through a man named Minister in Buckingham Street—"Minister of Grace" Rossetti dubbed him. He proceeded, according to William Michael, to fill up the house with "Chinese tables and chairs, Dutch tiles, Flemish and oriental and African curtains and draperies, looking glasses and mirrors of the seventeenth and eighteenth centuries, a chandelier here and another there, and numerous knick-knacks of whatever kind." William Michael described the routine in the early Cheyne Walk days:

> My brother's habits of an evening after the late dinner were quite antagonistic to any [literary] work on my part. Friends were very often with us, and much talk went on. . . . He lolled on the sofa, chatting as the humour came, or sometimes dozing. . . . My brother, though radically good natured, was not of what one calls an accommodating turn. His own convenience dictated his habits, and persons in his company had to adapt themselves as best they could. In those years . . . he did *nothing* in the evening, beyond talking and lounging . . . he wrote no more poems since the death of his wife, and the burial of his old poems in her coffin . . . he read no newspapers or periodicals, and was very seldom [seen] going carefully through a book. . . . We usually sat up late.

For the faithful William Michael, who had to be at his desk for the Inland Revenue at Somerset House every morning, it was sometimes a tiring regimen.

Swinburne was a tiny man with flaming red hair, subject to a nervous trembling that his contemporaries likened to St. Vitus's dance. He was a raging alcoholic and sexual exotic, who, naked, would indulge in frenzied dances, slide down staircase handrails, and generally create scenes. Drunk or sober, he loved to recite poetry. Henry Adams said Swinburne could recite a play of Sophocles or Shakespeare "forward or backwards from beginning to end." Georgiana Burne-Jones said that "when repeating poetry he had a perfectly natural way of lifting [his eyes] in a rapt, unconscious gaze, and their clear green colour softened by thick brown eyelashes was unforgettable." He is pictured here on the eve of the publication of his notorious *Poems and Ballads*, reading in manuscript to Gabriel and William "Anactoria," the poem which, along with the sado-masochistic "Dolores"—"Our Lady of Pain"—caused the greatest uproar. His friends had urged him not to publish the most pointedly offensive poems: Meredith, having heard "'low mutterings' from the lion of British prudery," advised him to "play savagely with a knife among the proofs for the sake of your fame"; Ruskin, to whom Swinburne read various poems, called them "some of the wickedest and splendidest verses ever written by a human creature"; William Michael and Gabriel also pleaded with Swinburne to be more cautious. Indeed Gabriel found even the private readings hard to take; he wrote to Tennyson (in a letter Max could not have known but seems to have intuited), "As no one delights more keenly in his genius than I do, I also have a right to say that no one has more strenuously combatted its wayward exercise in certain instances, to the extent of having repeatedly begged him not to read to me such portions of his writings when in MS." Undeterred, Swinburne went ahead, and in July 1866 published the book with Moxon. He went into a fit when he read its reception in the *Saturday Review*: the unnamed critic (in fact, John Morley) found it of no use to scold Swinburne for "grovelling down among the nameless shameless abominations which inspire him with such frenzied delight," as his is a mind "all aflame with the feverish carnality of a schoolboy over the dirtiest passage in Lemprière. It is not every poet who would ask us all to go hear him tuning his lyre in a stye . . . no language is too strong to condemn the mixed vileness and childishness of depicting the spurious passion of a putrescent imagination, the unnamed lusts of sated wantons, as if they were the crown of character and their enjoyment the great glory of human life. The only comfort about the present volume is that such a piece as 'Anactoria' will be unintelligible to a great many people." Swinburne, the review went on, seemed to think "there is really nothing in women worth singing about except 'quivering flanks' and 'splendid supple thighs', 'hot sweet throats' and 'hotter hands than fire', and their blood as 'hot wan wine of love'." The *London Review* said it would prefer "blank atheism" to Swinburne's perversions: "Anactoria" was "especially horrible," beginning with an "insane extravagance of passion" and ending with a "raging blasphemy." In the *Athenaeum*, the anonymous reviewer, actually Robert Buchanan, who later in his famous "Fleshly School" attack on Rossetti helped drive him to attempt suicide, called Swinburne "unclean for the mere sake of uncleanness. . . . Here, in fact, we have Gito [the homosexual boy in Petronius' *Satyricon*] seated in the tub of Diogenes, conscious of the filth and whining at the stars." All three reviews appeared on 4 August. The next day J. B. Payne, the head of Moxon, hearing a rumour of an even more severe review—if that were possible— planned by E. S. Dallas in *The Times*, and also fearing prosecution for obscenity, withdrew *Poems and Ballads* from circulation. Swinburne, with the help of Howell, got the book reissued immediately by John Camden Hotten, whose house publicly sold pirated editions of respectable American books and, secretly, erotic and pornographic books. At Hotten's urging,

Swinburne wrote a pamphlet in his own defence: he announced he was proud that "Anactoria" "has excited, among the chaste and candid critics of the day or hour or minute, a more vehement reprobation, a more virtuous horror, and a more passionate appeal, than any other of my writing." He thanked heaven that he was "evidently not virtuous enough to understand" what critics were reading into the poem, which was a "diluted and dilated form" of the spirit of Sappho's poem. What is so horrible, he asked, about paraphrasing Sappho, "the poem which English boys have to get by heart?"

And good-natured William Michael Rossetti, everybody's friend, went into print on Swinburne's behalf, calling "Anactoria" "one of the most glorious exhibitions of fervent imagination and poetic execution in his volume. The reader is not bound to like it: if he does not admire it, he has but a purblind perception of what poetic workmanship means. . . . The lesbian loves of Sappho [are] not germane to the modern mind. . . . Yet let not the artificer or the student of poetry be a mark for the mere mud of nineteenth-century highroads if some 'elective affinity' prompts him to penetrate somewhat further than parson or pedagogue into moods of mind and aberrations of passion which were vital enough to some of the great of old."

Herringham said of Swinburne:

He was the most childlike of little children. One did so want no harm to come to him. And he was so anxious to be good and obedient. But he hadn't will-power enough for that. He caused us all the greatest anxiety. What could be done? It wasn't that he drank much wine, but that so very little of it went to his head—and that he did always want a little. I fancy that somehow he *needed* it too. It wasn't good for his body; but then, you see, his body was such an infinitesimal part of him: the rest was all spirit; and the spirit perhaps required a special diet. . . . Meredith used to call him Algernon the Incalculable. "It's maddening," he would say, "to find one making so much out of—nothing. . . . We other fellows have to go through a long process of doing and *being*, and then of thinking hard about what we've done and what we are. We have to go to and fro, gathering faggots for tinder; laboriously and cunningly we stack them—and *then*, as likely as not, they won't burn. But Swinburne can always make a blaze without a speck of fuel. There is nothing *in* him but inspiration". . . . Another time, Meredith said, "It's all very well to say that Algernon gets his motive-power from books, not from life. It's true, but it's not the whole truth. If all the books in the world were burnt tomorrow, and nothing left of them but one charred corner of a page from an old French chronicle, Algernon would find enough in that to enable him to go on creating for ever."

Max's drawing, with its elongated candlestick, is a parody of Jacques Louis David's famous portrait of Madame Récamier.

12. GABRIEL AND CHRISTINA

Christina Rossetti, Gabriel's younger sister (the older, Maria, became an Anglican nun), gained a prominent place among the poets of her day with the publication of *Goblin Market* in 1862. She can be glimpsed in her youth as the sitter for Mary in Rossetti's *The Girlhood of Mary Virgin* (1849) and again in his *Annunciation* (1850). She was also one of the sitters for the face of Jesus in Hunt's *Light of the World* (1853). A deeply religious woman, Christina was twice engaged, once to the sleepy, timid painter James Collinson, a member of the Brotherhood, whose leanings towards Roman Catholicism could not be reconciled with her High but staunchly Protestant Anglicanism. She later refused the hand of Charles Cayley because he was a free thinker. She once left the room rather than be in the presence of Holman Hunt's second wife, his deceased wife's sister. Her almost morbid religiosity was exacerbated by ill health. (Virginia Woolf said Christina "positively liked being ill . . . it reminded her of her narrow bed, and of the chance of hell fire, and the probability of eternal torment.") Oddly enough, Swinburne and Christina got on very well; he was enormously fond of her, and late in life he dedicated one of his books to her. She read his *Atalanta in Calydon* (1865) with approval but pasted paper slips over offending passages, such as lines dealing with "the supreme evil, God."

Gabriel's reference to the singing bird and water shoot is from her 1857 poem "A Birthday":

> My heart is like a singing bird
>   Whose nest is in a watered shoot:
> My heart is like an apple tree
>   Whose boughs are bent with thickset fruit;
> My heart is like a rainbow shell
>   That paddles in a halcyon sea;
> My heart is gladder than all these
>   Because my love is come to me.

Raise me a dais of silk and down;
    Hang it with vair and purple dyes;
Carve it in doves and pomegranates,
    And peacocks with a hundred eyes;
Work it in gold and silver grapes,
    In leaves and silver fleurs-de-lys;
Because the birthday of my life
    Is come, my love is come to me.

13. GEORGE MEREDITH'S HORTATION

When Rossetti took the lease on 16 Cheyne Walk in October 1862, George Meredith became a part-time tenant, having a bedroom and sitting room for one night a week. Meredith had been under Rossetti's spell for a few years and was a friend of the other tenant, Swinburne. Rossetti had read in manuscript Meredith's *Modern Love* and encouraged him in the publication of that diagnosis of his unhappy marriage (to the daughter of Thomas Love Peacock, who had eloped with the painter Henry Wallis), and Swinburne had defended the poem in the pages of the *Spectator*. Meredith's accommodation at Cheyne Walk did not last long. As William Michael delicately put it, Meredith and Rossetti, while amicable and holding each other in "solid mutual regard," lacked towards each other "that thorough cordiality of give-and-take which oils the hinges of daily intercourse," and Meredith "found that Rossetti's arrangements, though ample for comfort of a more or less off-hand kind, were not conformable to his standard." Differing stories have come down about the last day of Meredith's tenancy: that Rossetti threatened to throw a cup of tea into Meredith's face if he repeated a remark, whereupon Meredith did so, Rossetti threw the tea, and Meredith stalked out; or, that Meredith departed after being disgusted at Rossetti's late breakfast at which he "devoured like an ogre five poached eggs that had slowly bled to death on five slabs of bacon." Whistler, much given to improving or inventing tales, said that Meredith had indiscreetly talked to a cabman about some disagreement with Rossetti, who, having heard of this from the cabman, announced at dinner that anyone gossiping with cabmen was not a gentleman. For emphasis Rossetti slapped down a serving spoon into the meat dish, squirting gravy into Whistler's face. Swinburne was reciting *Leaves of Grass*, and a wombat was eating from Gabriel's plate. It was all too much for the fastidious Meredith.

Half a dozen years later, Meredith told a friend about a few of Rossetti's habits: "Eleven a.m. plates of small-shop ham, thick cut, grisly with brine: four smashed eggs on it: work till dusk: dead tired on sofa till 10 p.m. Then to Evans' to dine off raw meat and stout. So on for years. Can Nature endure these things?" In 1909 Meredith felt obliged to state publicly that the words about breakfast were said in concern for his friend's health. He added, "I ventured to speak to him of the walk of at least a mile before this trying meal. But he disliked physical exercise."

Meredith, on the other hand, was a fanatic for exercise and loved the outdoors; he chopped down trees and sawed wood to improve his circulation; he especially liked spirited walks; a contemporary said of him that "he never merely walked, never lounged; he strode, he took giant strides." Herringham, in a paragraph that is an extended legend for Max's drawing, recalled:

Rossetti . . . the very sedentary Rossetti, found Meredith, with his great love of wind and weather, rather a trial. Rossetti had said one day dolefully, "He's always coming in early in the afternoon, just as I'm beginning to paint well.—'Glorious weather, Rossetti' he cries. 'Come out for a stretch with me—do you all the good in the world!' He always seems to be going to Hendon, and he always brings out the name as though it were a name to conjure with—something sacred, irresistible; Mecca; the Promised Land.—I say to him, Meredith, if you brought Hendon to me in your hand, I wouldn't look at it.—Or I say, Look here, my dear fellow: this is an easel, this is a canvas, this is a palette, and this is *me*—just getting into my stride. Go and get into yours, by all means. *I* don't ask you to sit down and help me paint this picture. Why should you want me to assist you in trapesing to Hendon? Once and for all, Meredith, Hendon be damned!—For a moment he has a puzzled look, then he throws back his head, laughs that great laugh of his, and swings out of the studio, banging the door behind him. I never dare ask him not to bang the door, because then he'd tell me that if I took exercise I shouldn't have nerves. And I should have to explain that I'd much rather jump an inch or two off my chair than walk ten miles or whatever the confounded distance to Hendon is."

Max had an almost inordinate regard for Meredith's writing, and he contrived to meet a few times with the then ancient survivor from mid-Victorian days. One of his visits took place just a week or two before the old man's death in May 1909. Max wrote: "Meredith was charming again. He seemed a little older than last year, but was just as full of talk and laughter. He seemed to have felt the death of Swinburne deeply. . . . He said he himself would soon be 'under the grass with the Prussians walking over him.' Also that three years of Prussianizing would do England a lot of good. He also had a scheme for a raid on France, to capture five hundred or so of French women, to brighten the breed of the future." When Meredith died, a dispute erupted: various people demanded he be buried in Poets' Corner, but the Dean of Westminster denied the request because Meredith had advocated five-year contracts for marriage. Nevertheless, the Dean, somewhat inconsistently, permitted a memorial service in the Abbey. Max's comment was "What a nation, or at any rate what a Dean." At the service Max saw another old survivor, Holman Hunt.

14. WILLIAM BELL SCOTT WONDERING

William Bell Scott, a painter and poet of small reputation, was one of Rossetti's closest and most faithful friends, from first to last. (Scott's long-time mistress, Alice Boyd, was also a friend.) Scott, although a much older man, certainly knew what it was that those fellows saw in Rossetti, he saw it himself. However, his posthumously published *Autobiographical Notes* (1892) had been frank about some of Rossetti's shortcomings; he said, for example, that Rossetti was not well adapted for married life, that marriage was "an even way of life the most unlikely possible to suit his late development." Thereupon Rossetti's champions, especially Swinburne (calling Scott "the parasite of the north") and Watts-Dunton, counter-attacked and made Scott appear a disgruntled outsider, jealous of Rossetti's fame. Max, with only these published accounts to follow, presents Scott in this erroneous light. It does not really matter; the picture conveys the mystery of Gabriel's magnetism. Of course that magnetism was strongest in the early years, before the increasing tendency of the late 1860s towards reclusiveness set in. Still, from the days of the Pre-Raphaelite Brotherhood in 1848 to those of the young idolizers that surrounded him at Oxford in 1857, from the first, happy, Cheyne Walk period to the last sad years of his life with its devoted watchers and protectors, Gabriel was king.

His faults were clear enough: he could be selfish, irresponsible, capricious, a spoiled child to whom friends were always catering. He was also sturdily stubborn; his friend William Allingham told, for example, how Gabriel would not hurry himself when late, remarking, "I never do anything I don't like." But there was no lack of disciples; as some would fall away, others would take their places. The testimony of some of the Oxford-Cheyne Walk circle is typical. Val Prinsep said: "To his friends he was very lovable, so much so that his very eccentricities became objects of idolatry . . . we had such an admiration for him that we even talked as he talked and used his very intonations. . . . Rossetti was the planet around which we revolved . . . we sank our own individuality in the strong personality of our adored Gabriel . . . to me he was as Pope and Emperor." Stanhope's niece wrote: "My uncle used to endorse the fact that among the banded talent of the Preraphaelites, Rossetti's was the master-mind which dominated the rest. No matter that all recognized him to be morally a man of lower ideals than themselves, the lure of his genius and his vivid personality conquered all who came in contact with it." To Burne-Jones' future wife, Rossetti's infectious cult of feminine beauty was "a new religion." To Burne-Jones, Rossetti was "the greatest man in Europe." Much later, Hall Caine, his last youthful disciple, would echo such sentiments, adding on his own that Rossetti had the singular faculty "of knowing things without taking the trouble to learn them, of seeing things without looking at them, of understanding things without thinking of them." Even the estranged William Morris, whose wife had been Rossetti's lover for many years, would say of the painter's death "It makes a hole in the world." For William Michael, Gabriel was "the pharos of our house." For Sylvester Herringham, Rossetti was, quite simply, "the best man I have ever known."

Max's drawing presents Rossetti's famous walled-in back garden, nearly an acre, where, in the early Cheyne Walk days he erected a large tent and held splendid, boisterous dinners. The yard was also the home of his notorious menagerie of "beasts." Rossetti's tastes in animals ran, William Michael said, to the "quaint, odd, or semi-grotesque": a Pomeranian, a great Irish deerhound, rabbits, dormice, hedgehogs, wombats, wood-chucks, marmots, armadilloes, kangaroos, wallabies, deer, white mice, racoons, squirrels, moles, peacocks, all sorts of owls. Stories have come down: the shrill trumpetings of the peacocks so annoyed neighbours that they prevailed upon Lord Cadogan, who owned most of the properties of the neighbourhood, that future leases contain clauses forbidding the keeping of peacocks; armadilloes burrowed away and popped up in neighbours' lawns, even on one occasion in a neighbour's kitchen; a racoon hibernated one winter in a drawer of Rossetti's Elizabethan wardrobe, and during the following spring its mysterious noises nearly convinced him the house was haunted; a small Brahmin bull, whose eyes, Whistler said, reminded Gabriel of Janey Morris's, was reported to have chased Rossetti around the garden. A wombat, a favorite (shown here snarling at Scott), was said to have died from eating cigars; and the kangaroos, mother and

son (one seen here being introduced to Rossetti by Morris) are recorded by
Treffry Dunn, Rossetti's painting assistant, as having met premature
deaths, the mother killed by the "bloodthirsty son," who was in turn
"polished off" by a racoon. Dunn maintained that Rossetti "had not any
great love for animals, nor knew much about their habits. It was simply a
passion he had for collecting, just as he had for books, pictures and china,
which impelled him to convert his house into a sort of miniature South
Kensington Museum and Zoo combined."

   In the drawing, in addition to Scott and Morris, Ford Madox Brown,
Burne-Jones, Swinburne, and possibly Walter Pater (the figure holding a
hat behind his back) are identifiable among Rossetti's disciples. An earlier
caricature, *Rossetti, in his Back Garden*, from *The Poets' Corner* (Supplementary plate 3), offers a much fuller cast of characters, including those
who visited at very different times, and one, Holman Hunt, who probably
never came to Cheyne Walk. The model is Fanny Cornforth.

15. Robert Browning introduces a Great Lady

Rossetti was an early, enthusiastic admirer of Browning's poetry. In 1847
he spotted the anonymous *Pauline* as Browning's and wrote to the poet
inquiring if he were correct. One of his criticisms of Paris when he visited it
as a young man in 1849 was that Browning's name was not known there.
Rossetti thought Browning like Shelley in lyrics, like Shakespeare in
drama. Browning, whose acquaintance Rossetti had made in 1852, called
fairly frequently at 16 Cheyne Walk. In Max's drawing, Browning's raised
thumb may suggest that touch of vulgarity some saw in him. The "Lady of
Rank and Fashion" cannot be positively identified, but it seems likely that
she is the exotic second Lady Ashburton. Born Louisa Mackenzie, she
married William Bingham Baring, Lord Ashburton, in 1858, the first Lady
Ashburton having died the previous year. (He was twenty-eight years older
than his second wife, and he died in 1864.) A woman of enormous wealth,
with a great interest in the arts, she owned paintings by Raphael, Titian,
and Rubens. She was also an open-handed patron of the arts: Lady Paget
said she was "generous, violent, rash and impulsive, ever swayed by the
impression of the moment. . . . Bevies of impecunious artists hovered about
her like locusts." A spectacular hostess to artists, writers, and other
notables, she attracted, among many others, Rossetti himself, who did some
sketches for her. Carlyle is said to have been in love with her, as he was
earlier in love with the first Lady Ashburton. In September 1869 Browning

asked for her hand in marriage, telling her, according to his own account, "my heart was buried in Florence [with Elizabeth Barrett Browning], and the attractiveness of a marriage with her lay in its advantage to Pen [his son]: two simple facts,—as I told her." Not surprisingly, she said no. Browning never forgave the bluntness of her refusal.

Browning also called frequently on Herringham, who, for Max's benefit, compared him to Tennyson:

> They were as unlike their own work as they were unlike each other. . . .
> The smoother Tennyson's verse became, the more rugged and tangled
> was he to look at. The more tangled and rugged Browning made his
> poetry, the more surely would anyone meeting him for the first time have
> taken him for a banker, or a fashionable physician. The greater the
> exactions he made, as he grew older, on the intellect and patience of his
> readers, the easier was it to understand what he said—and even to foretell
> what he *would* say—at a dinner-table. And Tennyson's manners—ah,
> they were the very least of all adapted to courtly circles at the very time
> when he had finally purged his art of anything that might conceivably vex
> the ghost of the Prince Consort.

Max's version of Browning, upon whom he never laid eyes, may have been influenced by Carlo Pellegrini's "Ape" caricature for *Vanity Fair* in 1875; but he seems also to have looked closely at the photograph widely circulated by the Browning Society in 1881. The Browning Society was founded in 1881 by that redoubtable organizer of scholarly activities, Frederick James Furnivall. He was one of the original projectors of what became the *Oxford English Dictionary*, and founder of the Early English Text Society, the Chaucer Society, the Ballad Society, and the New Shakespeare Society (in connection with which he engaged the irrepressible Swinburne in battle about Shakespearean scholarship, Furnivall labelling Swinburne "Pigsbrook" and Swinburne calling him "Flunkivall Brothelsbank"). Browning, who liked Furnivall personally and had served as nominal president of the New Shakespeare Society, laughingly agreed not to oppose a Browning Society. Furnivall's prospectus announcing the Society said that Browning was "*the* most thought-full" living poet; as for his notorious obscurity, "the Browning student will seek the shortcomings in himself rather than in his master." The Browning Society provoked much satire in the press, and there is no doubt that most of the members regarded Browning not merely as a great poet but as an oracle. Browning regarded the Society with an amused tolerance, along with gratitude for the boost it brought to the sales of his works. He avoided the Society's meetings but did occasionally, as in Max's caricature from *The Poets' Corner* (Supplementary plate 4), take tea with his worshippers.

16. George Augustus Sala with Rossetti

George Augustus Sala, a journalist and travel writer, worked for the *Daily Telegraph*, a penny paper claiming "the largest circulation in the world," and he became celebrated as their "Special Correspondent" during the American Civil War. Sala was a rather raffish, slightly vulgar man, a heavy drinker, one whom a contemporary, Francis Burnand, called "that king of Bohemians . . . the most brilliant, the most quaint, the wittiest, the kindest, and the most quarrelsome of them all." The Arundel Club, situated first in Salisbury Street, and then in Adelphi Terrace, Arundel Street, was known for its late hours and Bohemian clientele. T. H. S. Escott said it was founded by the theatrical writer Frank Talfourd "to add to his exhausting enjoyments and ensure against sufficient nightly rest." Talfourd, in Burnand's words, was "the most irregular of irregular livers, and the most careless," who "would dine when others breakfasted, and breakfast when other men dined"—habits much in keeping with Rossetti's own. At the Arundel Rossetti met Joseph Knight, who eventually published a *Life of Dante Gabriel Rossetti*, and W. S. Gilbert (Gabriel did not like him), who later aimed at him some of the satire in *Patience*.

J. M. Levy was proprietor of the *Daily Telegraph*. George Rae, a Birkenhead banker, and F. R. Leyland, a wealthy Liverpool shipowner, were patrons of Rossetti.

17. Swinburne and Mr. Gosse

Edmund Gosse first met Swinburne in 1871 at a gathering in Ford Madox Brown's hospitable house at 37 Fitzroy Square. Gosse, amid various oddly behaving guests—including Oliver Madox Brown carrying tame white rats on his arms and shoulders and the stout Gabriel squatting on a hassock at the feet of Janey Morris—riveted his attention on Swinburne, whom he had greatly admired for some years. In September 1867 Gosse, not quite eighteen, and not yet a full year up in London away from the fanatical evangelicalism of his father (so movingly commemorated in Gosse's *Father and Son*), wrote to Swinburne about poetry as a career, and received a friendly, if noncommittal, reply. During the next year he was shocked to see

Swinburne, whom he recognized from photographs, carried out unconscious from the Reading Room of the British Museum. Now they actually met, and Swinburne, Gosse recorded, "indulged me with quite a long conversation. His kindness, at once, became like the kindness of an elder brother. In some ways he fulfilled, and more than fulfilled, the promise of my hero-worship." Swinburne's pallid face, the balloon of red hair, the nervous movements that had him hopping up onto and down from the sofa were all "very strange." In later life Gosse became an authority on Swinburne, writing the poet's *DNB* entry and eventually publishing a lengthy *Life* that was much attacked for squeamishness. A. C. Benson said it was "the life of a fearless and ebullient little man, written by a man in an armchair who is afraid of everyone and everything," and Ezra Pound said it presented "a Swinburne coated with a veneer of British officialdom and decked out for a psalm-singing audience."

Max's drawing of Swinburne taking Gosse to see Rossetti came to Gosse's attention in 1917 when the Rossetti caricatures were first exhibited. Gosse wrote rhapsodically to Max: "You have never done anything more irradiated with genius than this new Rossetti series." Gosse's favourite drawings, he told Max, were the Brown and Hunt, Swinburne reading "Anactoria," Watts, Shields, and Caine, and the Jowett. "*My* picture," Gosse continued, "was a startling surprise . . . I had not reached it, when I heard a gentleman say to a lady 'The Gosse is very funny!' I think the little red fairy Swinburne tugging my impassiveness along, stamping and swinging with impatience, is beyond praise. Genius, simply, and divination—which is the flower and summit of your genius. It was very kind of you . . . to drag me into the scheme." Max had met Gosse in 1896, they had become friends, and the older man, who encouraged many young writers, came to think of himself, mistakenly, as Max's literary mentor. Perhaps that is why Max, who made many caricatures of Gosse, always drew him looking rather like a schoolmaster.

18. MR. MORLEY BRINGS MR. MILL

John Morley, here a youngish man of 31, editor of the *Fortnightly Review* (a journal to which Rossetti twice contributed), with his distinguished career as statesman and man of letters still in the distant future, introduces a frail John Stuart Mill to Rossetti. It is doubtful that even illustrations by Rossetti would have mitigated the violent abuse that the publication of *The Subjection of Women* generated in the press.

Herringham claimed that the Pre-Raphaelites "owed much" to Mill and Spencer, to Utilitarianism and Philistinism, because these drove the Pre-Raphaelites in upon themselves and kept them from being "spoilt."

In 1917 Morley published his self-praising *Recollections*, and Max late in the same year gave to E. V. Lucas, for a Red Cross benefit sale at Christie's, a manuscript entitled "Further Recollections by Viscount M. O.M." Max insisted at the time that it not be published: "One doesn't want to run the risk of hurting the feelings of a good (and with a slight effort one might almost say great) old man." Morley, who had been made Viscount Morley of Blackburn (his birth place) in 1908, died in 1923. His "Further Recollections," which concern a visit he paid to Rossetti at Cheyne Walk in 1871 (Morley oddly enough calling it his only meeting with the painter), are published for the first time as Appendix 4.

19. Mr. Leighton suggests Candidature

Frederic Leighton, a highly successful painter and active Academician, the handsome "Adonis of the Galleries," entreats Rossetti to join the Royal Academy. Rossetti's response to this Man from Hymettus, that is, from the Greek mountain known for its honey, is readily predictable from his customary recumbent position on the sofa. For one thing, the Pre-Raphaelite Brotherhood had been founded in rebellion against the Academy. And in his later years Rossetti became so reclusive that he seldom went anywhere or stirred himself in matters other than his own art. Moreover, he rarely exhibited his paintings. The President of the Royal Academy, whom Leighton calls "not of all men the most enlightened" was Sir Francis Grant, elected in 1866, a portrait painter whose great interests were hunting and high life. William Bell Scott, attacking the Royal Academy in the *Gentleman's Magazine* in 1877, told the story that Grant, when offered a Sanzio, that is, a Raphael, for an Old Masters exhibition, refused it, saying, "Well gentlemen . . . we want the pictures of great masters, you know; as for Sanzio, I never heard of him." Leighton himself succeeded Grant as President in 1878, to be followed in turn by Millais in 1896.

20. MR. WATTS, MR. SHIELDS, AND MR. CAINE

Hall Caine, a young man apprenticed to a Liverpool architect but burning with literary ambitions, first wrote to Rossetti in 1879, telling the ailing painter/poet of a lecture in which he had defended him. Encouraged by friendly letters from Rossetti, Caine visited Cheyne Walk in 1880, and in 1881 he was invited to live in the house as a companion and secretary. For his services he received bed and board and the thrill of entry into artistic, Bohemian London. Caine was with Rossetti almost continually until the painter's death on Easter Sunday, 9 April 1882, at the seaside village of Birchington, Kent. Also with Rossetti at the end were two devoted followers, Frederick Shields, painter and close friend, and Theodore Watts, later Watts-Dunton, solicitor turned critic. For the few years preceding Rossetti's death, Shields and Watts had been constant in attendance, and they may have had their doubts about the newcomer Caine. The title to Max's drawing, "*Quis Custodiet. . .*" is adapted from Juvenal: Who will guard the guard himself? Caine's "luridly arresting" novels were of a much later date.

Sometime in 1881 Herringham met his estranged friend Rossetti, and the two were apparently on the verge of making up: "But you see," Herringham told Max, "we were not alone. There was the small man—I forget his name, but I gathered he was acting as a sort of companion or nurse—bright red hair—and I remember hearing later that he became a very popular novelist. . . . He said something about Mr. R's work now appealing to a wider and ever wider public. He said something about 'phenomenal sales' and something about 'the heart of every man and every woman in the English-speaking world—' I caught Rossetti's eye, and I thought I saw there for an instant a gleam of the great old laughter. . . . I never saw him again."

Of the numerous memoirists who sprang into print about Rossetti after his death, Caine was among the very first, in a self-serving book that Max detested. He "persecuted" Caine in articles and caricatures, and was much embarrassed one morning in 1902 to meet unexpectedly, at his brother's house, Caine himself. He had become a popular religious novelist; in Max's words, he had "rushed . . . into the market-place and chartered a cart and a trumpet and the biggest drum that ever was made." In reviewing Caine's *The Christian* for the *Daily Mail* in August 1897, Max prefaced his murderous slating of the book by protesting that Caine's preliminary puffings of his novel were not, as some had alleged, a disgrace to literature: "One should be grateful to any man who makes himself ridiculous."

The drawing of Rossetti and his three guardians offers Max's most detailed presentation of the crowded interior of 16 Cheyne Walk. On the wall are paintings of Jane Morris and, quite prominently, a circular mirror. When Treffry Dunn first visited Cheyne Walk and was ushered into the sitting room, "mirrors of all shapes, sizes and designs, lined the walls, so that whichever way I gazed I saw myself looking at myself." William Michael, describing the furnishings of the house, remarked that Rossetti "had a particular liking for convex round-shaped mirrors." Max, on reading these two witnesses, must have been heartened. He himself owned a convex mirror, originally purchased by his father at the Paris Exhibition of 1867, and it was part of Max's life from his nursery days until his death. A convex mirror, Max said, had poetry: "by miniaturizing, it concentrates and essentializes." Rossetti, according to Herringham, "loved *mirror*" and called Herringham's convex mirror "the only artist among mirrors— emphasising and attenuating—always a composition—*Rondure*—the aim of all art." (Morris, on the other hand, hated mirrors: "They lie—you can see a thing straight for yourself.")

Two years before Hall Caine came to live at Cheyne Walk, Watts-Dunton had rescued Swinburne from drink and probably from death by taking him into his suburban house at Putney. There Swinburne lived a tame if uncreative existence until his death in 1909. Max, invited by Watts-Dunton in 1899 to visit and meet Swinburne, recorded how at lunch, a sober Swinburne "smiled . . . to himself, and to his plateful of meat, and to the small bottle of Bass's pale ale that stood before him—ultimate allowance of one who had erst clashed cymbals in Naxos. This small bottle he eyed often and with enthusiasm, seeming to waver between the rapture of broaching it now and the grandeur of having it to look forward to."* Max's meeting with Swinburne thrilled him and inspired his best-known essay, "No. 2, The Pines" and a splendid caricature, *At the Pines* (Supplementary plate 6). For Beerbohm, Swinburne was Catullus, still alive, and lodging in the suburbs. The marvel was not merely length of years but that he seemed altogether of another age: "He was and would always be that flammiferous boy of the dim past—a legendary creature,

---

*Watts-Dunton had weaned Swinburne from brandy to port to Burgundy to claret and finally to "the wine of the country," English beer. In addition to the small bottle at lunch, Swinburne was permitted, during his morning walk, one glass of beer at a local pub. Philip Guedalla in *Bonnet and Shawl* (1928) included an imaginary account of how Swinburne in the 1880s married—without Watts-Dunton's approval—Sophia Grimes, barmaid of the Mortlake Arms in the Richmond Road (see Supplementary plate 5). In reality, it was Watts-Dunton who disturbed the bachelor arrangements of the two men, by marrying, in 1905, a woman more than fifty years younger than himself.

sole kin to the phoenix. . . . He was a singing bird that could build no nest. He was a youth who could not afford to age." Max, in barely contained excitement, entered the house:

No. 2—prosaic description! But as that front-door closed behind me I had the instant sense of having slipped away from the harsh light of the ordinary and contemporary into the dimness of an odd, august past. Here, in this dark hall, the past was the present. Here loomed vivid and vital on the walls those women of Rossetti whom I had known but as shades. Familiar to me in small reproductions by photogravure, here they *themselves* were, life-sized, "with curled-up lips and amorous hair" done in the original warm crayon.

Watts-Dunton met him first, talking of having much work on hand. What that work was remained a mystery, "a part of the dear little old man; it went with the something gnome-like about his swarthiness and chubbiness—went with the shaggy hair that fell over the collar of his eternally crumpled frock-coat, the shaggy eyebrows that overhung his bright little brown eyes, the shaggy moustache that hid his small round chin." And Swinburne:

Here, suddenly visible in the flesh, was the legendary being and divine singer. Here he was . . . a strange small figure in grey, having an air at once noble and roguish, proud and skittish. . . . Almost the first impression he made on me . . . was that of a very great gentleman indeed. Not of an *old* gentleman, either. Sparse and straggling though the grey hair was that fringed the immense pale dome of his head, and venerably haloed though he was for me by his greatness, there was yet about him something— boyish? girlish? childish, rather; something of a beautifully well-bred child. But he had the eyes of a god, and the smile of an elf. In figure, at first glance, he seemed almost fat; but this was merely because of the way he carried himself, with his long neck strained so tightly back that he all receded from the waist upwards. . . . So small and sloping were his shoulders that [his] jacket seemed ever so likely to slip right off. . . . His hands were tiny, even for his size, and they fluttered helplessly, touchingly, unceasingly.

Staring down at the two survivors, and at the intruder from posterity, is Rossetti's *Reverie*, or rather Max's version of that picture, an 1868 coloured chalk portrait of Jane Morris.

21. THE TOUCH OF A VANISHED HAND

Charles Augustus Howell, known as "Owl" to his friends, was an adventurer of Anglo-Portuguese origin who acted as agent and factotum for writers and artists, most notably Ruskin, Swinburne, Rossetti, G. F. Watts, Burne-Jones, Madox Brown, Frederick Sandys, and Whistler. All felt the enchantment of his personality, his humorous talk, his opportunistic business sense. Whistler called him "the wonderful man, the genius, the superb liar, the Gil-Blas, Robinson-Crusoe hero out of his proper time, the creature of top-boots and plumes—splendidly flamboyant." (After the famous trial in which Ruskin, accused of libel for writing that Whistler was "flinging a pot of paint in the public's face," had been found guilty but fined only a farthing in damages, Howell complained that had he been called as witness, he could have "really" won the case. "Yes," replied Whistler, "you would have won and we would all have been in Newgate!") But Howell eventually fell out with everyone for whom he acted, being accused of all sorts of villainy, from making empty promises to outright lying, from stealing to forging works of art. To Swinburne he became "the pole-cat Howell" for telling stories of Swinburne's private indecencies and for pawning his incriminating letters. Howell's break with Burne-Jones, who enjoyed a reputation for sturdy marital conventionality, seems to have been caused by his bringing together the painter's wife, Georgiana, and his Greek model, Mrs. Mary Zambaco, with whom Burne-Jones was having an affair.

In 1857 the then seventeen-year-old Howell was introduced to Rossetti. Shortly thereafter he became vaguely implicated in the Orsini conspiracy to assassinate Napoleon III, and had to flee England; he returned in 1864, with half-invented stories of adventures with sunken galleons, of living as a sheik in Morocco, and of work for the Portuguese embassy in Rome. By 1865 he renewed his acquaintance with Rossetti and began to undertake tasks for him. It was to Howell that Rossetti entrusted the exhumation of Lizzie's grave to recover his buried poems. As Rossetti told his brother, he did not know "anyone except Howell who could well have been entrusted with such a trying task." Howell arranged many painting commissions for Rossetti, and even William Michael, who would not return to friendship with Howell after Rossetti's death, admitted that Howell was "unsurpassable" in business dealings for his brother. But Howell sometimes promised more than he could deliver, and Rossetti accepted commissions he failed to execute. Howell was dismissed as Rossetti's agent in 1876, on the accumulated score of Howell's recent unsanctioned arrangements with a patron, overcharges for models' dresses, and an unreturned pearl pin Rossetti had lent him. Nonetheless, Rossetti harboured no grudge, in spite of his later conviction that Howell had forged some paintings of his. Shortly before his death Rossetti was heartened by a visit from Howell to Birchington where he lay grievously ill. Hall Caine recorded:

> "And what are you doing now, Charles?" said Rossetti.
>
> "Buying horses for the King of Portugal," said the soldier of fortune, and then Rossetti laughed until he nearly rolled out of his seat.
>
> Our visitor stayed all day, telling stories, veracious and apocryphal, of nearly everybody known to us in the world . . . the visit of this unaccountable being did him good, and he laughed all evening after the man had gone.

Howell, though devoted in his fashion to his wife and child, was nonetheless a ladies' man. Whistler said he was "like a great Portuguese cock of the poultry yard: hens were always clucking about him." Foremost among these was Rosa Corder, a painter of horses and dogs, who was Howell's mistress for many years and who bore him a child he brought up as his "niece." In Max's drawing Rosa Corder, alleged to have assisted Howell in earlier forgeries of Rossetti, is perpetuating "the touch of a vanished hand" (a phrase from Tennyson's "Break, Break, Break") by copying Rossetti's *Bocca Baciata*, "Kissed Mouth," portrait of Fanny Cornforth.

Herringham related:

> I once said to Rossetti, "If I were you, I wouldn't see so much of [Howell]. I don't think he's to be trusted." Rossetti laughed. "Sylvester," he said, "whenever a man says to me *If I were you*, I pay no attention, because I know that what he means is *If you were I*; and because I happen to be myself. If I happened to be you, I daresay I should forbid Howell the door, and live in terror of him, and surround myself with a loyal bodyguard of dreadful dullards. You're young, Sylvester. When you're as old as I am, you'll realize it's the *dull* friends that one has to avoid, not the untrustworthy ones. You'll come to me and say in a hollow voice, *If I were you, I wouldn't see so much of So-and-So: He's dull.* And I shall look up and say, *Is he? Why I do believe you're right! Yes, I'm conscious that he's been exhausting me all this time. Many thanks for your warning.*—A man who's got work to do, Sylvester, can't afford not to have amusing people about him. Charles Howell is the most amusing fellow I know. He gives me something all the time. As for the off-chance of his doing me a mischief round the corner—

why, that's all the more reason for not letting him out of my sight. I must see more of Howell."

It was Howell who in 1872 arranged that the Prince of Wales visit 16 Cheyne Walk, with the result that his Royal Highness sat to Rossetti for *Princeps Triplumiferus*, that "little-known portrait in oils" (Supplementary plate 7), in the vain hope of meeting Mrs. Morris.

22. Rossetti's Name is Heard in America

Oscar Wilde, a close but not intimate friend of Max's in the 1890s, and a definite influence on his writing, is the subject of the last caricature in *Rossetti and His Circle*. The drawing forms a kind of coda to the book and connects Rossetti's world to Max's own. Wilde greatly admired Rossetti and in some ways the aesthetic movement which he stood for was heir to Pre-Raphaelitism and the artistic world that centered round Rossetti. Wilde, *mutatis mutandis*, was the Rossetti of his day. The two men never met; indeed Rossetti disliked the aesthetes and was much annoyed at Wilde's tribute to him in his first volume of poems (1881). In April 1881 Gilbert and Sullivan's *Patience* appeared on the London stage, satirizing aestheticism. Bunthorne, the "Fleshly Poet," contained features of Rossetti, Swinburne, and Wilde, but the public immediately identified the character with Wilde. When *Patience* later opened in New York, the producer thought it good publicity to have Wilde lecture in America. Wilde spent all of 1882 in America, lecturing continually across the country. He was generally well received.

Max's drawing shows Wilde, in the aesthetic dress he wore while delivering his talk "The English Renaissance," explaining to his listeners that aesthetic young men in England used the lily as a "perfect model of design," especially in the decorative arts, and not, in spite of Mr. Gilbert, as food.

Wilde also said:

And these Pre-Raphaelites, what were they? If you ask nine-tenths of the British public . . . you will hear some thing about an eccentric lot of young men to whom a sort of divine crookedness and holy awkwardness in drawing were the chief objects of art. To know nothing about their great men is one of the necessary elements of English education. . . . In England, then as now, it was enough for a man to try and produce any serious beautiful work to lose all his rights as a citizen; and besides this, the Pre-

Raphaelite Brotherhood . . . had on their side three things that the English public never forgives: youth, power and enthusiasm.

Satire, always as sterile as it is shameful and as impotent as it is insolent, paid them that usual homage which mediocrity pays to genius—doing, here as always, infinite harm to the public, blinding them to what is beautiful, teaching them that irreverence which is the source of all vileness and narrowness of life, but harming the artist not at all, rather confirming him in the perfect rightness of his work and ambition. For to disagree with three-fourths of the British public on all points is one of the first elements of sanity, one of the deepest consolations in all moments of spiritual doubt.

Rossetti, stirring his heavy bottom on the sofa (as Bell Scott once described him), would have nodded or grunted or smiled.

*   *   *

The drawings that became *Rossetti and His Circle* were purchased by Mrs. Charles Hunter, widow of an immensely wealthy coal magnate and hostess to many artists and writers. In November 1917 she lent fifteen of the drawings to the Modern Loan Exhibition at the Grosvenor Gallery. The exhibition, much of it deriving from Mrs. Hunter's collection, was an important show of modern art, and included English and American painters whom Max loved to caricature, Steer, Conder, Sickert, Augustus John, Sargent, Whistler, Tonks; but also Degas, Rodin, and Fantin Latour. Max, in England at the time, must have been pleased to have been the only caricaturist in the company.

In September 1921 the Leicester Galleries, which had acquired the drawings, exhibited all twenty-three (along with drawings and paintings by the Pre-Raphaelites and others), whereupon they were purchased for 800 guineas by Hugh Walpole, an insatiable collector of art. In 1923 Walpole lent the series to the Tate Gallery for an exhibition called *Paintings and Drawings of the 1860s Period*. While the Pre-Raphaelites could hardly have been said to be in vogue at the time, the exhibition, which included 334 works by Rossetti, Millais, Burne-Jones, Arthur Hughes, Elizabeth Siddal, Holman Hunt, Frederick Sandys, George Boyce, and others, was impressively large. Among Millais's oils, *Ferdinand Lured by Ariel* was prominent (*Cherry Ripe*, that momentary vision that once befell Millais as he painted the Pre-Raphaelite picture, was not there). As in the Grosvenor

Gallery and Leicester Gallery exhibitions earlier, Max was again the only caricaturist to be represented.

In 1938 Walpole, lunching in his home at 90 Piccadilly with John Rothenstein, recently appointed Director of the Tate Gallery, suddenly and unexpectedly declared that after his death Rothenstein could select for the Tate whatever he wanted from Walpole's collection. They decided Rothenstein should name fourteen paintings. What about Max's twenty-three Rossetti drawings, already lent to the Gallery? "Oh, count them as one item," said Walpole. And thus the *Rossetti and His Circle* caricatures (along with oils by Renoir, Forain, Steer, Sickert, John, Tissot, Ford Madox Brown, drawings by Blake and John, and a watercolour by Cézanne) became, in 1941, the property of the nation.

The series of drawings, called "Rossetti and his Friends" in the 1917 and 1921 exhibitions, was published as *Rossetti and His Circle* by William Heinemann in September 1922. It was more properly a "book" than Max's other collections of caricatures because of its unity of theme, story line, and indispensable legends. The printing consisted of 3,500 copies, 1,000 of which went to the U.S.A. The book cost 25s. Heinemann issued simultaneously a De Luxe Edition of 300 copies, in a white buckram cover, each copy numbered and signed by the author, and priced at three guineas. For this Yale University Press edition, the first since Heinemann's, the drawings have been photographed anew from the originals in the Tate Gallery. The colours of the 1922 edition were primitive and artificially harsh; Max dealt chiefly in soft subtle washes. The reproductions for the new edition are somewhat larger than those in the first edition (the actual drawings vary in size from *Rossetti's Courtship*, approximately 13 by 8 inches, to *Rossetti's Name is heard in America*, approximately 16 by 15 inches). An attempt has been made to echo the type and format of the original, over which Max, as for all his books, exercised a fussy and tyrannical control.

Seven supplementary plates have been added in the section called, after one of Max's own provocative book titles, "More." Additional, appendix-like materials are placed in the section "And Even More." Included here is a list of "Books Old and New." The old ones helped Max. All of them have helped me and will prove useful to those who wish to investigate on their own the world of Rossetti and his circle and more especially that "silver thread of lunacy" which, as Max said, ran so delightfully through "the rich golden fabric of 16 Cheyne Walk."

ROSSETTI
AND HIS CIRCLE

NOTE

Anxious to avoid all occasion of offence, I do hope this book will not be taken as a slight to men of the moment. Throughout the past quarter of a century I have been proclaiming by pencil my great interest in such men; and the only fault I have found in them is that (numerous though they always are) they are not numerous enough to satisfy my interest in mankind. They would suffice me if I were properly keen on metaphysics, Chippendale, the beauties of Nature, the latest discoveries in science, the shortest cut to Utopia, etc. I don't agree that the proper study of mankind is Man. I do but confess that Man is the study that has been most congenial to me—so congenial that the current specimens of him have always whetted my appetite for other ones. Lack of imagination debars me from the pleasure of gazing much at the great Jones who is to leave so deep an impress on the late twentieth century, and the even greater Robinson who is to loom so tremendously, for good or evil, over the thirtieth. It is to the Past that I have ever had recourse from the Present. Years ago there was a book entitled *The Poets' Corner*, in which some of my adventures into the Past were recorded by me. But in that volume there was a slight admixture of the (then) Present. In this latest volume there is nothing of anything that wasn't the Past when I was a child. Hence the apologetic (but not, I hope, abject) tone of these prefatory words.

Perhaps I ought also to beg your pardon for having here confined myself to one little bit of the Past. In *The Poets' Corner* I ranged back as far as Homer. Here I haven't so much as shown Rossetti before he passed out of baby-clothes into breeches. Perhaps you have never heard of Rossetti. In this case, I must apologise still more profusely. But even you, flushed though you are with the pride of youth, must have heard of the Victorian Era. Rossetti belonged to that—though he was indeed born nine years before it began, and died of it nineteen years before it was over. For him the eighteen-fifties-and-sixties had no romance at all. For me, I confess, they are very romantic—partly because I wasn't alive in them, and partly because Rossetti was.

Byron, Disraeli, and Rossetti—these seem to me the three most interesting men that England had in the nineteenth century. England had plenty of greater men. Shelley, for example, was a far finer poet than Byron. But he was not in himself interesting: he was just a crystal-clear crank. To be interesting, a man must be complex and elusive. And I rather fancy it must be a great advantage for him to have been born outside his proper time and place. Disraeli, as Grand Vizir to some Sultan, in a bygone age, mightn't have seemed so very remarkable after all. Nor might Rossetti in the Quattrocento and by the Arno. But in London, in the great days of a deep, smug, thick, rich, drab, industrial complacency, Rossetti shone, for the men and women who knew him, with the ambiguous light of a red torch somewhere in a dense fog. And so he still shines for me.

It does not appear that the men and women who knew him well were many. But the men atoned for their fewness by a great deal of genius, and the women by a great deal of beauty. Rossetti had invented a type of beauty; otherwise perhaps we should not be regarding these ladies as beautiful. And certainly the genius of the younger men would not but for him have expressed itself just as it did. Holman Hunt, Millais, Swinburne, Morris, were among those whose early work bore his stamp. Burne-Jones' work bore it always. Even Whistler's had it for a time. These men, with a sprinkling of remarkable elder and younger persons who at one time and another entered or at any rate impinged on the magic Circle, you will find in the pages of this book. Rather a ribald book? Well, *on se moque de ce qu'on aime*. And besides, there is no lack of antidotes. I refer you to William Rossetti's biography of his brother—a very thorough piece of work, full of well-ordered facts, and very pleasant in tone. Holman Hunt's autobiography is a finely solid and (between the lines) delightful production. Professor Mackail's book about Morris is a penetrating work of art. Nor could a husband and his friends be portrayed more vividly and prettily than Burne-Jones and his friends were portrayed by his widow. And if, albeit earnest, you are in a great hurry, there is always the Dictionary of National Biography, you know.

I must warn you, before parting, not to regard as perfectly authentic any of the portraits that I here present to you. Rossetti "to my gaze was ne'er vouchsafed." Nor did I ever set eyes on Coventry Patmore or Ford Madox

Brown or John Ruskin or Robert Browning. Nor did I see any one of the others until he had long passed the age at which he knew Rossetti. Old drawings and paintings, early photographs, and the accounts of eye-witnesses, have not, however, been my only aids. I have had another and surer aid, of the most curious kind imaginable. And some day I will tell you all about it, if you would care to hear.

M. B.

Rapallo, 1922.

FRONTISPIECE

D. G. ROSSETTI, PRECOCIOUSLY MANIFESTING, AMONG THE EXILED PATRIOTS WHO FREQUENTED HIS FATHER'S HOUSE IN CHARLOTTE STREET, THAT QUEER INDIFFERENCE TO POLITICS WHICH MARKED HIM IN HIS PRIME AND HIS DECLINE.

D. G. Rossetti, previously mentioned, among the titled patrons who frequented his father's home in Charlotte Street, felt grave indifference to politics which marked him in his prime and his decline.

1. BRITISH STOCK AND ALIEN INSPIRATION, 1849.

FIRST COUNTY MEMBER
HOLMAN HUNT

"Very clever, no doubt—"

SECOND COUNTY MEMBER
JOHN MILLAIS

"Full of wonderful ideas, but—"

FIRST COUNTY MEMBER
SECOND COUNTY MEMBER
HOLMAN HUNT
JOHN MILLAIS

"Not to be trusted for one moment."

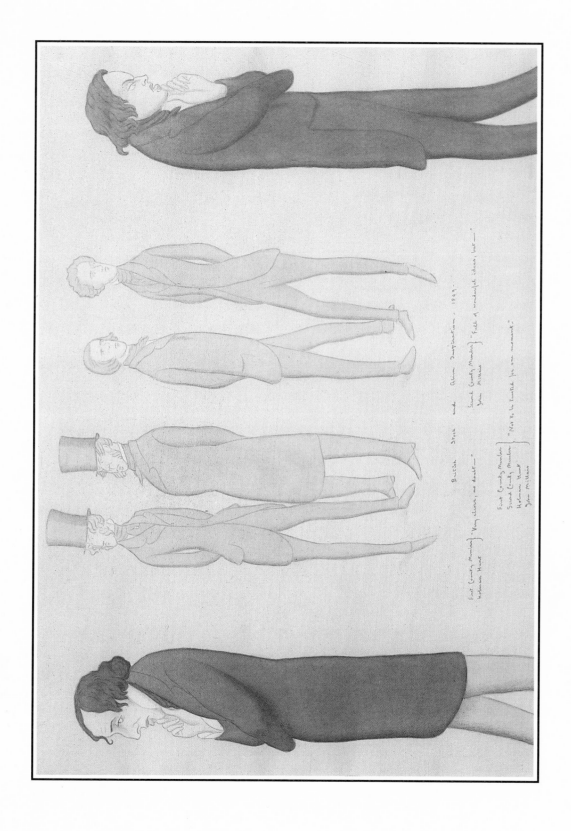

2. Rossetti's Courtship. Chatham Place, 1850–1860.

Rosetti's Courtship — Chatham Place, 1850–1860.

3. A Momentary Vision that once befell Young Millais.

4. The sole remark likely to have been made by Benjamin Jowett about the mural paintings at the Oxford Union.

"And what were they going to do with the Grail when they found it, Mr. Rossetti?"

The sole remark likely to have been made by Benjamin Jowett about the mural paintings at the Oxford Union?

"And what were they going to do with the Grail when they found it, Mr Rossetti?"

5. Spring Cottage, Hampstead, 1860.

Coventry Patmore very vehemently preaches to the Rossettis that a tea-pot is not worshipful for its form and colour, but as a sublime symbol of domesticity.

6. Topsy and Ned Jones, settled on the settle in Red Lion Square.

7. An Introduction.

Miss Cornforth: "Oh, very pleased to meet Mr. Ruskin, I'm sure."

Miss Cornforth: "Oh, very pleased to meet Mr. Ruskin, I'm sure."

8. BLUE CHINA.

9. Woolner at Farringford, 1857.

Mrs. Tennyson: "You know, Mr. Woolner, I'm one of the most un-meddlesome of women; but—when (I'm only asking), *when* do you begin modelling his halo?"

Woolner at Farringford, 1857—

Mrs. Tennyson: "You know, Mr. Woolner, I'm the most un-meddlesome of women, but — When (I'm only asking) when do you begin modelling his halo?"

10. FORD MADOX BROWN BEING PATRONISED BY HOLMAN HUNT.

Ford Madox Brown being patronised by Holman Hunt. max 1916

11. The Small Hours in the 'Sixties at 16, Cheyne Walk.—Algernon reading "Anactoria" to Gabriel and William.

The Beadles shown in the "Sixties at 16 Chepow Walks. — Aldgrower author (manuscript) to Gerard and Williams.

12. Rossetti, having just had a fresh consignment of "stunning" fabrics from that new shop in Regent Street, tries hard to prevail on his younger sister to accept at any rate one of these and have a dress made of it from designs to be furnished by himself.

D. G. R. "What *is* the use, Christina, of having a heart like a singing bird and a water-shoot and all the rest of it, if you insist on getting yourself up like a pew-opener?"

C. R. "Well, Gabriel, I don't know—I'm sure you yourself always dress very quietly."

Rossetti, having just had a fresh consignment of "stunning" fabrics from that new shop in Regent Street, tries hard to prevail on his younger sister to accept at any rate one of these and have a dress made of it from designs to be furnished by himself.

D. G. R. "What is the use, Christina, of having a heart like a singing-bird and a water-shoot and all the rest of it, if you insist on getting yourself up like a pew-opener?"

C. R., "Well, Gabriel, I don't know, I'm sure you yourself always dress very simply."

13. Rossetti insistently exhorted by George Meredith to come forth into the glorious sun and wind for a walk to Hendon and beyond. Autumn 1862.

14. Mr. William Bell Scott wondering what it is those fellows seem to see in Gabriel.

15. Mr. Browning brings a lady of rank and fashion to see Mr. Rossetti.

16. ROSSETTI IN HIS WORLDLIER DAYS (*CIRCA* 1866–1868) LEAVING THE ARUNDEL CLUB WITH GEORGE AUGUSTUS SALA.

MR. SALA: "You and I, Rossetti, we like and we understand each other. Bohemians, both of us, to the core, we take the world as we find it. *I* give Mr. Levy what *he* wants, and *you* give Mr. Rae and Mr. Leyland what *they* want, and glad we are to pocket the cash and foregather at the Arundel."

Rossetti, in his worldlier days (circa 1866–1868) leaving the Arundel Club with George Augustus Sala.

Mr Sala's "You and I, Rossetti, we like and we understand each other: Bohemians, both of us, to the core, we take the world as we find it; and is for our work, I give Mr Levy what he wants, and you give Mr Rae and Mr Leyland what they want; and glad we are to pocket the cash, and forgathering at the 'Arundel'."

⌈ The moralising is academical, but not so the acquaintance. — M.B. ⌉

17. Riverside Scene.

Algernon Swinburne taking his great new friend Gosse to see Gabriel Rossetti.

Riverside Scene —

Algernon Swinburne taking his great new friend Gosse to see Gabriel Rossetti —

max 1916

18. Mr. Morley of Blackburn, on an afternoon in the Spring of '69, introduces Mr. John Stuart Mill.

"It has recently," he says, "occurred to Mr. Mill that in his lifelong endeavour to catch and keep the ear of the nation he has been hampered by a certain deficiency in—well, in warmth, in colour, in rich charm. I have told him that this deficiency (I do not regard it as a defect) might possibly be remedied by *you*. Mr. Mill has in the press at this moment a new work, entitled 'The Subjection of Women.' From my slight acquaintance with you, and from all that I have seen and heard of your work, I gather that women greatly interest you, and I have no doubt that you are incensed at their subjection. Mr. Mill has brought his proof-sheets with him. He will read them to you. I believe, and he takes my word for it, that a series of illustrative paintings by you would" etc., etc.

Mr. Morley of Blackburn, on an afternoon in the Spring of '69, introduces Mr. John Stuart Mill. "It has recently," he says, "occurred to Mr. Mill that in his life-long endeavour to catch and keep the ear of the nation he has been hampered by a certain deficiency in — well, in warmth, in colour, in rich charm. I have told him that this deficiency (I do not regard it as a defect) might possibly be remedied by you. Mr. Mill has in the press at this moment a new work, entitled 'The Subjection of Women'. From my slight acquaintance with you, and from all that I have seen and heard of your work, I gather the women greatly interest you, and I have no doubt you are incensed by their subjection. Mr. Mill has brought his proof-sheets with him. He will read them to you. I believe, and he takes my word for it, that a series of illustrative paintings by you would" etc. etc.

19. A Man from Hymettus.

Mr. Frederic Leighton: "Think not for one moment, my dear Mr. Rossetti, that I am insensible to the charm of a life secluded, as yours is, from the dust of the arena, from the mire of the market-place. Ah no!—I envy you your ivory tower. How often at some Council Meeting of the R.A. have I murmured within me that phrase of Wordsworth's, 'The world is too much with us'. But alas! in all of us there is a duality of nature. You, *O felix nimium*, are singer as well as painter. I, separated from my easel, am but a citizen. And the civistic passion—yes, passion, dear Mr. Rossetti—restrains the instinct of the artist in me towards solitude, and curbs the panting of the hart in me for the water-brooks. I feel that I have, in conjunction with my colleagues, a duty to the nation. To improve the taste of the Sovereign, the taste of her ever-genial first-born and of his sweet and gracious consort, of the Lords Spiritual and Temporal and of the faithful Commons, of the Judicial Bench, of those who direct the Army and Navy and Reserve Forces, of our merchant princes in Threadneedle Street and of our squires in the Shires, and through all these to bring light and improvement to those toiling millions on whom ultimately the glory of Great Britain rests—all this is in me an ambition not to be stifled and an aspiration not to be foregone. You smile, Mr. Rossetti, yet I am not disemboldened to say now, as I have often wished to say to you, in the words of the Apostle Paul, 'Come over and help us!' Our President—I grant you in confidence—is not of all men the most enlightened. But I, in virtue of what is left to me of youth and ardour, conjoined with the paltry gift of tact, have some little influence in Burlington House. Come now!—let me put your name down in our Candidates' Book."

A Man from Hymettus.

Mr. Frederic Leighton: "Think not, for a moment, my dear Mr. Rossetti, that I am insensible to the charm of a life secluded, as yours is, from the dust of the arena, from the mire of the market-place. Ah no!—I envy you your ivory tower. How often at some council meeting of the R.A. have I echoed within me that phrase of Wordsworth's, "The world is too much with us." But alas! in all of us there is a duality of nature. You, O filio minimo, are singer as well as painter. I, regarded from my easel, am but a citizen. And the civistic passion—yes, passion, dear Mr. Rossetti—restrains the impulse of the artist in me towards solitude and curbs the panting of the heart in me for the water-brooks. I feel that I have, in conjunction with my colleagues, a duty to the nation. To impose the taste of the Sovereign, the taste of her ever-gracious first-born and his sweet and gracious consort, of the Lords Spiritual and Temporal and of the faithful Commons, of the Judicial Bench, of those who direct the Army and Navy and the Reserve Forces, of our merchant princes in Threadneedle Street and of our squires in the shires, and through all these to bring light and improvement to those toiling millions on whom ultimately the glory of Great Britain rests—all this is in me an ambition not to stifled and an aspiration not to be forgone. You smile, Mr. Rossetti, yet I am not disembosaned to say how, as I have often wished to say to you, in the words of the Apostle Paul, "Come over and help us." Our President—I grant you in confidence—is not at all even the most enlightened; but I, in virtue of what is left to me of youth and ardour, conjoined with the mellow cult of fact, have some little influence in Burlington House. Come now!—let me put your name down in our Candidates' Book."

20. *Quis Custodiet Ipsum Custodem?*

Theodore Watts: "Mr. Caine, a word with you! Shields and I have been talking matters over, and we are agreed that to-night and henceforth you *must* not and *shall* not read any more of your literary efforts to our friend. They are too—what shall I say?—too luridly arresting, and are the allies of insomnia."

Quis Custodiet Ipsum Custodum?

Theodore Watts: "Mr. Caine, a word with you! Shields and I have been talking matters over, and we are
agreed that this evening and henceforth you must not and shall not read any more of your literary
efforts to our friend. They are too — what shall I say? — Too luridly arresting, and are the
allies of insomnia."

21. MR. ——— AND MISS ——— NERVOUSLY PERPETUAT-
ING THE TOUCH OF A VANISHED HAND.

22. THE NAME OF DANTE GABRIEL ROSSETTI IS HEARD FOR THE FIRST TIME IN THE WESTERN STATES OF AMERICA. TIME: 1882. LECTURER: MR. OSCAR WILDE.

MORE

1. Swinburne, Elizabeth Siddal, and Rossetti.

2. Mr. Tennyson reading *In Memoriam* to his Sovereign.

3. Dante Gabriel Rossetti, in his back garden.

Rossetti, Whistler, Swinburne, Watts-Dunton, Meredith, Burne-Jones, Morris, Hall Caine, Hunt, Ruskin, Fanny Cornforth.

4. MR. ROBERT BROWNING, taking tea with the BROWNING SOCIETY.

5. SWINBURNE AND MISS SOPHIA GRIMES.

6. At the Pines.

7. PRINCEPS TRIPLUMIFERUS

A little-known portrait in oils of Edward VII (then Prince of Wales) by D. G.
Rossetti. Circa 1873.

It appears to have appeared to Mr. Charles Augustus Howell that his illustrious
friend would be able to command even higher prices if his work were sealed with
the approval of some really fashionable member of the Reigning House. He
bethought him of the Prince of Wales. As usual, his resourcefulness was more than a
match for difficulties. On such-and-such an afternoon of the following week the
Prince's brougham drew up sharp at the wrought-iron gate of 16, Cheyne Walk.
His Royal Highness was escorted by Mr. Rossetti and by Mr. Howell to the
drawing-room, where he partook of the sandwiches and other refreshments that
had been sent on previously in a hamper from Marlborough House. It would seem
that he was, as always, full of affability and bonhomie, and rather more than
usually brilliant – though mainly of course in that interrogative vein of which he
was a master. He enquired whether Mr. Hhwossetti were an Italian; whether he
did not think that the shape of Italy on the map was very like that of a boot; when
he had first come to London; *where* he was born in London; whether his father still
lived at that addhhwess; *when* and of *what* his father had died; how old his mother
was; how it was that so many of the organ-ghhwinders in London were Italians;
whether the monkeys on the organs were Italian monkeys; whether it were not
more difficult to paint in oils than in water-colour; the date of the invention of oil-
paints; what Mr. Hhwossetti was laughing at; whether he knew Sir Charles
Eastlake; whether . . . but this page would not contain a tithe of the searching
questions that His Royal Highness put, punctuating the replies with that deep-
throated *What-what* or *Yess-yess-yess* which is so affectionately remembered by all
who were privileged to come near him.

The brief meal having been consumed, an adjournment was made to the Studio,
where his Royal Highness held a review of Mr. Rossetti's recent work, including La
Ghirlandata, Sibylla Palmifera, Reverie, Water-Willow and many others. It
appears that he criticised these from a human, rather than from a merely technical,
standpoint, and expressed a particular wish to meet Mrs. Morris. He said that he
had asked a few friends to dine with him next Sunday at the Star and Garter, and
that he would be pleased to include that lady among his guests. It was explained to
him by Mr. Howell that Mr. Morris was a man of uncouth and headstrong nature,
with leanings to Republicanism, Monogamy, and other damnable heresies, and
that really his wife went nowhere. It was said by Mr. Howell that her sole privilege
was that whenever Mr. Rossetti was well on with a new portrait—when he had
had (say) seven sittings—Mrs. Morris was allowed by her husband to come and
superintend with her counsel the later stages of the work.

It does not appear that she appeared at the eighth or any other sittings accorded
by the Prince to Mr. Rossetti; and it does appear that at length these sittings
terminated somewhat abruptly—the Prince declaring forcibly (as had so often
before, and has so often since, been declared by lesser men) that Mr. Howell's word
was inferior to his bond. Be this as it may, the portrait had been finished. It is one of
the best examples of Rossetti's later and more luscious manner, an altogether
admirable likeness, and an enduring monument not less to the genius of Mr.
Howell than to the early prime of Edward, the Peace-Giver.

Much of the beauty of the work is, alas, lost here through the limitations of the
three-colour process.

AND EVEN MORE

DANTE GABRIEL ROSSETTI, 1863
Photograph by Lewis Carroll.

ALGERNON CHARLES SWINBURNE, DANTE GABRIEL
ROSSETTI, FANNY CORNFORTH, WILLIAM MICHAEL
ROSSETTI, 1863.

Photograph by William Downey.

WILLIAM BELL SCOTT, JOHN RUSKIN, DANTE GABRIEL
ROSSETTI, 1863.

Photograph by William Downey.

SYLVESTER HERRINGHAM VAINLY ENDEAVOURING TO ENLIST
D. G. R.'S INTEREST IN SOME SINGULARLY INTERESTING
EXPERIMENT.

"THE MIRROR OF THE PAST" MANUSCRIPT PAGE

Swinburne, W. M. Rossetti, Ford Madox Brown, William Bell Scott, Elizabeth
Siddal, Tennyson, and Ruskin with Rossetti.

"The Mirror of the Past," manuscript page

Jane Burden, Rossetti, Ruth Herbert, Elizabeth Siddal.

SYLVESTER HERRINGHAM ON WILLIAM MORRIS AS DECORATOR

Of William Morris at the time when he had founded with his friend Faulkner the famous firm of furnishers and decorators, Herringham gave me an interesting glimpse: "One morning Pringle, my butler, came up to my study and said that Mr. Faulkner and another gentleman were in the drawing-room. He said, 'I told Mr. Faulkner you were not at home, sir, but the other gentleman said that then they'd come in and wait.' I asked Pringle who the gentleman was. 'I don't know, sir,' he said. 'A sea-faring gentleman, I think.' I wondered what Morris could want with me.

"As I went downstairs I heard his voice raised in great enthusiasm about something, and, as I entered, the sturdy and rosy fellow rushed at me and clapped me on the shoulders. 'Splendid,' he cried, stepping back, 'grandiose, scrumptious.'

"'What is?' I asked.

"'Why, this,' he answered, spinning round on his heel, with his right arm extended, and radiantly facing me again.

"'You like the room?' I asked.

"'Like it? Why, it's the most beautiful room in London.'

"I turned to Faulkner (who was standing in the background—looking, I noticed, rather uncomfortable) and 'Well,' I said, 'this *is* praise indeed from Sir Hubert! I was afraid Morris wouldn't approve of my taste at all. This sofa, for instance—very different from that famous wooden settle of his in Red Lion Square.'

"'Sofa?' cried Morris. 'Call that a sofa? Why it's only a—a perch for canary-birds. But the *room*—Golly!' and he spun ecstatically round on his heel, upsetting this time a slim Sheraton stand on which was a silver vase with a rose in it. 'Sorry,' he exclaimed, picked up the stand, re-placed the vase and the rose, and—he was always extraordinarily handy—mopped the wet floor dry with his huge handkerchief; all in an instant of time. 'Sorry,' he said again, 'but it's the gimcrack's own fault, you know. And it clinches our scheme, by Jove, doesn't it?'

"'What scheme?' I inquired.

"'Oh, I forgot: you weren't in the room. *The* scheme. To make a clean sweep of all these folderols and really *furnish* the room. Moment I came in, I swore we'd do this *for* you—didn't I, Faulkner? We'd been round to see Gabriel Rossetti, on business. As we came away Faulkner pointed out this house to me—told me you lived here. Confess I'd quite forgotten you, old chap. Liked the look of your house, though. Thought you might want some things. Besides: pleasure to see you again. Wasn't prepared for this room, though. Felt the challenge of it at once. I've got half the designs in my head already, and I'll put 'em in hand today. All you've got to do is to get your things carted off to Christie's or somewhere and pocket what they fetch. I and Faulkner and Co. will do the rest.'

"I said, 'Your idea is that I should sell all that I have and follow you?'

"'Right!—you've hit it,' he cried. 'And what's more, we'll let you have everything at two per cent above cost of production, by Jiminy, because we're blooming beginners and you're our friend. Hooray! I've got *all* the designs in my head now,' and he struck his forehead a violent blow with his fist. 'I see your whole blessed room for you, all clear before me. You shall have a great cedar chair—*there*, in the middle—like Odin's throne; and a settle—all along *this* wall—to seat a regiment. And Ned Burne-Jones will do the stained glass for your windows—Life of La Belle Iseult; and Ford Madox Brown shall do the panels of the settle—Boyhood of Chaucer; and'—he strode up and down, brandishing his arms—'there's a young chap named William De Morgan who'll do the tiles for the hearth; and my wife shall embroider the edges of the window-curtains—you know that green serge we've got, Faulkner—glorious. And by Jove we'll'—but here he slipped and sat with a terrific crash on the parquet. 'That's just what I was going to speak about,' he continued, sitting; 'this isn't a floor, it's a sheet of ice: it won't do; we must have good honest rough oaken boards with bulrushes,' he cried, bounding to his feet, '—strewn bulrushes. And we'll have a—'

"'One moment, Morris,' I begged. 'When you say *we*, do you mean simply yourself and Faulkner and the Company, or do you include *me*?'

"'But of course I include you,' he said. 'Why, hang it all, the *room*'s yours.'

"'That's just what I was beginning to doubt,' I said.

"He stared hard at me, and I at him. Rather a dog-and-cat effect, I suppose. It lasted some seconds. Morris saw that I wouldn't waver. One of his great qualities was that he never wasted time. He always concentrated his energies on things that *could* be done, he never repined over things that couldn't. Here was a thing that couldn't. He looked at his watch, whistled (he always whistled whenever he looked at his watch), snatched his hat—

'Come along, Faulkner!' he cried. 'No offence, Herringham!'—and was gone.

"He was a queer fellow—a great character; quite apart. And as good as gold. But I hadn't much in common with him."

FURTHER RECOLLECTIONS BY VISCOUNT MORLEY O. M.

Chapter I

We will admit that in certain crafts and callings a high degree of proficiency may be attained without exercise of the strictly cerebrative faculties.—STODDART.

It is a right counsel for Princes that they should investigate the minds of humbler persons.—MACHIAVELLI.

"*Primae impressiones nonnumquam optimae.*" The phrase occurs in an encyclical by a Pontiff of whom it was unkindly but not untruly said by a well-known Roumanian critic in the eighteenth century that the world owed less to him than to the bulk of his predecessors. Nevertheless, the phrase itself strikes true, and I feel I am right in not omitting from these pages the name of a certain poet and painter, famous in his day, whom I saw but once. In the summer of 1871, through the intermediacy of a younger but still more famous poet who was his friend, I had secured the promise of an article by him on the Relation of Poetry to Painting for the periodical which I had the honour to edit. Time passed, and the MS. of D. G. Rossetti did not reach me. S[winburne] bade me exercise that virtue which was said by a great leader of men in ancient days to be the most essential of all. But patience, carried beyond a certain point, is itself a form of laxity, as Joubert well said. One afternoon in the late autumn I set a firm foot on Rossetti's doorstep.

Apart from the matter of my errand, I was not incurious to see him. I was, it is true, no fervent admirer of his poems, published in the previous year. I had missed in that hot-house the keen bite of the Blackburn air. There was something cloying in all that nectar to one nurtured like myself on the pure milk of J. S. Mill's doctrine. I had not (a most significant abstention) committed any of his verses to memory. But I felt that in his known cult for the greatest of Florentine poets we had a bond of union. There is, I like to think, a tang of Blackburn in all that Dante wrote; and I had recently learnt by heart five-hundred lines of the Divina Commedia. These, soon after I was shown into the studio, I recited to Rossetti. I may be forgiven for remembering that he complimented me on my accent; which he said was quite perfect, and declared (in jest) that my real name must be Giovanni Morli. During the recitation he had gone on painting from his model, a certain Mrs. E[lephant], who all the time seemed to be on the verge of laughter, evidently supposing that the Commedia was a comedy in the English sense of that word. A pretty woman, but dressed in a costume of some colour which I remember striking me as over-bright. Rossetti himself a civil and agreeable fellow. Rather less than the medium height, I fancy, but in this I may be mistaken. "*Chacun*," said a shrewd observer, "*mesure la stature des autres selon la sienne*," and I, though in the comic prints I have sometimes been portrayed as short, am in reality tall. I remember a dinner at the house of E. Marjoribanks, given soon after I took office under Mr. G[ladstone]. The talk turned on the proverbial difficulty of gauging heights. Our host sent for a yard-measure, and presently measured us, one after another, against a door. "And what," I asked, after the operation had been performed on my person, "am *I*?" E. M. "Six foot three." J. M. "I should have guessed somewhat less." E. M. "Well, you would have been wrong." At this, a certain well-known sculptor, who was of the party, said, "He looks less because he is so perfectly proportioned." I mentioned this remark subsequently to Herbert Spencer, on his death-bed. He said that it raised an interesting point in anthropometry, and made a note of it in pencil. That is my justification, if such be needed, for mentioning it here.

In the course of my talk with Rossetti I asked what he thought of the comment made by a certain critic, well-versed in letters and in affairs, on re-reading in later life Burke's complete works: How admirable! The greatest man since Milton. D. G. R. "Did Burke write anything?" J. M. "Assuredly." D. G. R. "I should have thought he was too busy." After some cross-purposes it became clear that the painter thought I had referred to a certain garroter who had been well-known in the previous decade. He said he had never heard of "this other fellow," and as for Milton, was of opinion that poetry ought always to be "amusing," and that Milton's was not. I lost the calm that is habitual to me, left the studio hurriedly, and realised a moment later that I had forgotten my hat. Returning for it, I found the painter executing a sort of heavy but wild dance in the middle of the room. He stopped short at sight of me, and explained after a moment that as his work kept him so much indoors he had to take his exercise in that form.

Outside in Cheyne Walk I paused to lean over the parapet. A strong northerly wind had sprung up, blowing straight from Blackburn, and troubling the surface of the river, which flowed full and strong, with a swirl at the bridges. Dark clouds scudded overhead. Day was nearing its end. The lamps along the embankment were already lit, gleaming pale and ineffective like the ideas of some great statesman in an age not ready for them. These pensive scenes are the true background of our life and thought, the external setting of our human things. I watched the barges as they breasted the tide. An unforgettable hour. Slowly I made my way eastward, under a heavy shower of rain.

I heard some time later, and I hope I may be forgiven for recalling, that Rossetti declared me to have a more richly-nourished mind than any man he had ever met, a larger outlook, a deeper insight, a greater command of the right words. It seems also—and I note it as a possible instance of that "care for inessential things" attributed to women by an Asiatic writer well-known in his day—that Mrs. E[lephant] said my eyes were the loveliest she had ever seen.

Dec. 1917

BOOKS OLD AND NEW

Behrman, S. N. *Portrait of Max: An Intimate Memoir of Sir Max Beerbohm*. New York: Random House, 1960.

Burne-Jones, Georgiana. *Memorials of Edward Burne-Jones*. 2 Vols. London: Macmillan & Co., 1904.

Caine, Hall. *Recollections of Dante Gabriel Rossetti*. London: Elliot Stock, 1882.

Cecil, David. *Max: A Biography*. London: Constable, 1964.

Cline, C. L. [ed.] *The Owl and the Rossettis: Letters of Charles A. Howell and Dante Gabriel, Christina and William Michael Rossetti*. University Park; London: Pennsylvania State University Press, 1978.

Danson, Lawrence. *Max Beerbohm and The Mirror of the Past*. Princeton: Princeton University Library, 1982.

Doughty, Oswald. *A Victorian Romantic: Dante Gabriel Rossetti*. London: Frederick Muller, 1949.

Dunn, Henry Treffry. *Recollections of Dante Gabriel Rossetti and His Circle (Cheyne Walk Life)*. Edited and annotated by Gale Pedrick, with a prefatory note by William Michael Rossetti. London: Elkin Mathews, 1904.

Felsteiner, John. *The Lies of Art: Max Beerbohm's Parody and Caricature*. New York: Knopf, 1972.

Fredeman, William E. *The Letters of Pictor Ignotus: William Bell Scott's Correspondence with Alice Boyd, 1859–1884*. Manchester: The John Rylands Library, 1976.

— *Prelude to the Last Decade: Dante Gabriel Rossetti in the Summer of 1872*. Manchester: The John Rylands Library, 1971.

— *Pre-Raphaelitism: A Bibliocritical Study*. Cambridge: Harvard University Press, 1965.

Gosse, Edmund. *The Life of Algernon Charles Swinburne*. London: Macmillan & Co., 1917.

Grushow, Ira. *The Imaginary Reminiscences of Sir Max Beerbohm*. Athens, Ohio: Ohio University Press, 1984.

Hart-Davis, Rupert. *A Catalogue of the Caricatures of Max Beerbohm*. London: Macmillan, 1972.

— *Hugh Walpole: A Biography*. London: Macmillan, 1952.

— [ed.] *The Letters of Oscar Wilde*. London: R. Hart-Davis, 1962.

Hunt, William Holman. *Pre-Raphaelitism and the Pre-Raphaelite Brotherhood*. 2 Vols. London: Macmillan & Co., 1905.

Hyder, Clyde K. [ed.] *Swinburne: The Critical Heritage*. London: Routledge & Kegan Paul, 1970.

Irvine, William, and Park Honan. *The Book, the Ring, & the Poet: A Biography of Robert Browning*. New York: McGraw-Hill, 1974.

Lutyens, Mary, and Malcolm Warner [eds.]. *Rainy Days at Brig o' Turk: The Highland Sketchbooks of John Everett Millais*. Westerham, Kent: Dalrymple Press, 1983.

Mackail, J. W. *The Life of William Morris*. 2 Vols. London: Longmans & Co., 1899.

McMullen, Roy. *Victorian Outsider: A Biography of J. A. M. Whistler*. New York: E. P. Dutton, 1973.

Martin, Robert Bernard. *Tennyson: The Unquiet Heart*. Oxford: Clarendon Press, 1980.

Minto, W. [ed.] *Autobiographical Notes of the Life of William Bell Scott . . . and Notices of his Artistic and Poetic Circle of Friends, 1830 to 1882*. 2 Vols. London: Osgood, McIlvaine & Co., 1892.

Ormond, Leonée. *Tennyson and Thomas Woolner*. Lincoln: The Tennyson Society, 1981.

Pennell, E. R. & J. *The Whistler Journal*. Philadelphia: J. B. Lippincott Co., 1921.

Peterson, William S. *Interrogating the Oracle: A History of the London Browning Society*. Athens, Ohio: Ohio University Press, 1969.

Rossetti, William Michael. *Dante Gabriel Rossetti: His Family-Letters: With a Memoir by W. M. Rossetti*. 2 Vols. London: Ellis & Elvey, 1895.

— *Some Reminiscences of William Michael Rossetti*. 2 Vols. London: Brown, Langham & Co., 1906.

Stevenson, Lionel. *The Ordeal of George Meredith: A Biography*. New York: Scribners, 1953.

Surtees, Virginia. *The Paintings and Drawings of Dante Gabriel Rossetti (1828–1882): A Catalogue Raisonné*. 2 Vols. Oxford: Clarendon Press, 1971.

Thomas, Donald. *Swinburne: The Poet in his World*. London: Weidenfeld and Nicolson, 1979.

Thwaite, Ann. *Edmund Gosse: A Literary Landscape, 1849–1928*. London: Secker & Warburg, 1984.

Watts-Dunton, Theodore. *Old Familiar Faces*. London: Herbert Jenkins, 1916.

Weintraub, Stanley. *Four Rossettis: A Victorian Biography*. New York: Weybright and Talley, 1977.

Woolner, Amy. *Thomas Woolner, R.A., Sculptor and Poet: His Life in Letters*. London: Chapman & Hall, 1917.

Viscusi, Robert. *Max Beerbohm, or The Dandy Dante*. Baltimore and London: The Johns Hopkins University Press, 1986.